The V.

CENTENARY CLASSICS

Original publication dates of reprinted titles are given in brackets

Joseph Johnston, *Civil War in Ulster* (1913)
Darrel Figgis, *A Chronicle of Jails* (1917)
Ernie O'Malley, *Rising Out* (2007)
Padraig de Burca and John F. Boyle, *Free State or Republic?* (1922)
Mossie Harnett, *Victory and Woe* (2002)
P. S. O'Hegarty, *The Victory of Sinn Féin* (1924)

The Victory of Sinn Féin

✦

P.S. O'HEGARTY

*with a series introduction by Fearghal McGarry
and an introduction by Tom Garvin*

UNIVERSITY COLLEGE DUBLIN PRESS
Preas Choláiste Ollscoile Bhaile Átha Cliath

First published in 1924
First published in 2010 by
University College Dublin Press
Centenary Classics Edition 2015
© Bríghid Bean uí Éigeartaigh 2015
Series Introduction © Fearghal McGarry 2015
Introduction © Tom Garvin 2015

ISBN 978-1-906359-99-7
ISSN 2009-8073

University College Dublin Press
UCD Humanities Institute, Room H103
Belfield, Dublin 4
www.ucdpress.ie

CIP data available from the British Library

Typeset in Scotland in Ehrhardt by Ryan Shiels
Text design by Lyn Davies, Frome, Somerset, England
Printed in Dublin on acid-free paper
by SPRINT-print

CONTENTS

CENTENARY CLASSICS SERIES INTRODUCTION

Fearghal McGarry

'The true history of a passionate period,' wrote P. S. O'Hegarty in *The Victory of Sinn Féin* in 1924, 'cannot be written by any contemporary. We are all too near it.' How does the revolutionary period appear from our present perspective, one hundred years after the Easter Rising? And, now that we have an abundance of 'the necessary documents and data' that O'Hegarty thought essential to write a balanced history, what do the voices of those who lived through this era have to tell us?

Although inevitably shaped by the period in which it was written, the historiography that has emerged over the past century has gradually transformed our understanding of the Irish revolution. The earliest accounts were mostly written by republicans. Popular memoirs by IRA leaders such as Dan Breen and Tom Barry, or the *Fighting Stories* recorded by Irish Volunteers throughout the country, often presented the conflict as a straightforward struggle between the Irish people and the malign forces of British imperialism. The Civil War was frequently overlooked, as were the perspectives of those who did not experience the preceding 'Four Glorious Years' as a period of liberation. This republican narrative was reinforced by school textbooks, as well as by State commemoration which centred on the sacrificial gesture of Easter 1916 rather than the more divisive violence that followed.

From the 1970s, when professional historians belatedly turned their attention to the period, more sophisticated and critical interpretations emerged. Local histories presented a more complex picture of the forces that shaped the conflict. Revisionist accounts emphasised social and political divisions rather than unity, and explored how factors other than patriotism, such as generational conflict, collective pressures and rising social frustrations, motivated many. Against the backdrop of the Northern Irish Troubles, the acrimonious debates that followed revealed a gulf between popular assumptions and scholarly perspectives.

Despite recent controversies centred on revolutionary violence in Cork, this gap has narrowed considerably, as is demonstrated by the transformation of attitudes to Irish soldiers in the Great War. The emergence of a more nuanced understanding of the past is also evidenced by the changing nature of State commemoration (even if this also reflects new imperatives resulting from the Good Friday Agreement, including a problematic tendency to understate past enmities). Notwithstanding criticism of aspects of the government's commemorative programme, the adoption of a 'decade of centenaries' incorporating the campaign for Home Rule, and Irish experiences of the Great War, alongside the War of Independence has enabled a more pluralistic approach than previous major commemorations. So too has the greater attention focused on the role of labour, women and campaigns for social reform.

Another positive development is the widening of access to contemporary sources through such projects as the digitisation of the Military Service Pensions Collection and the 1901–11 Census. Complementing these initiatives, UCD Press's new 'Centenary Classics' series makes available eye-witness accounts of key revolutionary episodes including the Ulster crisis; the aftermath of 1916;

the rise of Sinn Féin; the War of Independence; the Treaty split; and the Civil War. These provide first-hand perspectives on such topics as the significance of sectarian divisions; the impact of imprisonment on republicanism; the importance of popular mobilisation and guerrilla warfare; and the conflict's divisive legacy.

Although most historical controversies stemming from the revolutionary era focus on republican agency, Joseph Johnston's *Civil War in Ulster* reminds us how Ireland was plunged into crisis during a period when republicans exercised little influence. His account of the Home Rule crisis illustrates the role played by Ulster unionists, supported by powerful allies in Britain, in destabilising Ireland before the First World War. Ulster unionist defiance of Westminster, the formation of the Ulster Volunteer Force, and the establishment of a provisional government in Belfast exposed the limitations of the Liberals' Irish policy, not least its self-interested failure to reconcile the democratic demand of Irish nationalists for self-government with the right of Ulster's unionists to determine their own future. The divided loyalties of the British army in Ireland, exemplified by the Curragh mutiny of March 1914; the double standards of the police, seen in the contrasting responses to gun-running in Larne and Howth; and the undermining of the British Government by a Tory party whose incendiary rhetoric and support for armed resistance in Ulster verged on treason, contributed to the failure to achieve a peaceful settlement of the Irish question. Although sometimes interpreted as an irrational response to the Easter Rising, the collapse of popular support for Home Rule can only be understood within the wider context of the Ulster crisis, and the subsequent impact of the Great War.

Like that of other contemporaries (such as the Irish republicans enthused by the Orangemen's success in arming themselves), the perspective of Joseph Johnston – a liberal Ulster Protestant who believed his people could be won round to Home Rule – now seems naïve. However, his repudiation of the Ulster Unionist claim that civil war in Ulster was preferable to the modest reforms represented by Home Rule seems less so, particularly in the context of the 'Home Rule all round' that many expected (and which has since come to pass). In present-day Northern Ireland, where communal identities remain no less entrenched a century later, contemporary resonances can be discerned: the difficulties of sustaining support for political compromise; the pull of sectarian forces towards instability; and the appeal of intransigence, despite its counter-productive consequences, still appear relevant lessons from history.

These accounts offer many insights into the influences that shaped the revolutionary generation. The significance of the cultural nationalist revival is repeatedly encountered. The importance attached to history is particularly striking. The influence of books such as John Mitchel's *Jail Journal* and *Speeches from the Dock*; stories of 1798 and 1867; and memories of the Famine and Land War, is evident, as is the importance of commemoration, most notably of the 1798 centenary which contributed to a wider political revival leading to the formation of Sinn Féin. For republicans like Mossie Harnett and Seán Connolly, the emotional power of the story of Ireland was reinforced by its links with family and local tradition. Much of the success of the Easter rebels resulted from their appropriation of this insurrectionary tradition, and their ability to present it as a viable strategy rather than a vestige of the romantic past.

Marketed as a modern-day *Jail Journal*, Darrell Figgis's memoir of imprisonment also illustrates the republican claim to continuity. As was the case with mid-nineteenth-century Fenianism, propaganda and self-sacrifice were at least as important as revolutionary deeds in cultivating popular support. The first evidence of the republican movement's growing popularity was the success of the campaigns, largely run by women, in support of the 1916 prisoners. The executions of the Rising's leaders, and the subsequent death of imprisoned martyrs such as Thomas Ashe and Terence MacSwiney, reinforced the idea of Britain as draconian and vindictive, and of the insurrectionary tradition as a timeless struggle against tyranny.

The 'cementing of brotherhood' in Frongoch and British jails shaped the emergence of a coherent republican movement. Imprisonment could, as for Michael Collins, enhance one's political prospects or – as with Figgis and Eoin MacNeill – salvage a career blemished by failure to turn out in 1916. Conflicts within the prisons, and the wider support they generated, demonstrate the importance of non-violent struggle after 1916. However, like other aspects of the popular mobilisation achieved by Sinn Féin – the by-elections of 1917–18, the anti-conscription campaign of April 1918, the General Election of 1918 and the establishment of Dáil Éireann in January 1919 – political activism came to be eclipsed by the armed struggle of 1919–21. Revealingly, in contrast to earlier periods when glorious failure and sacrifice were all that could be celebrated, the heroism of IRA memoirs came to overshadow the tragic appeal of prison literature.

The military dimension of the War of Independence is explored closely by two books in this series. Ernie O'Malley's account of Seán Connolly's IRA activities in the midlands and west, and Mossie Harnett's memoir of his experiences as O/C of the West Limerick Brigade's 2nd Battalion, convey the experiences of regional commanders, dealing candidly with the difficult subject matter of ambushes, executions, and the challenges of sustaining support for a campaign of guerrilla warfare. Harnett's account of his service with the anti-Treaty IRA is particularly valuable given his generation's reticence on the Civil War.

Dying for freedom – as Seán Connolly, along with five of his comrades, did at Selton Hill – also entailed killing for Ireland. The price of violence forms a central theme of P. S. O'Hegarty's *The Victory of Sinn Féin* which spans the years between 1916 and 1923.

Believing that politics rather than force should have determined the course of events after the Rising, O'Hegarty attributed the 'moral collapse' of the Irish people to the rise of the cult of the gunman and the horrors of war. Despite O'Hegarty's bleak Treatyite outlook, Harnett's account, conveying his own disillusionment with politics, illuminates many of the same concerns from a different perspective. In particular, the IRA's belief that the politicians had squandered the victory achieved by the gun contributed to the tragic events that followed the War of Independence.

The Treaty debates form the focus of Padraig de Burca and John F. Boyle's *Free State or Republic?* Based on their press reports for the *Irish Independent*, their account complements the spare (and sometimes tediously detailed) transcripts of the debates which are now available on the website of the Oireachtas. Like other first-hand sources, it conveys a sense of what it felt like to be there at the time, describing the changing mood in the chamber, the demeanour of the deputies, the manner in which they delivered their speeches, and their impact; de Valera's words, 'which electrified the assembly', clearly resonated in the Dáil in a way that they do not on the page, a reminder of a charisma of sorts lost to time. The debates divided those who advocated the Treaty as a stepping stone to full independence from those who rejected, largely on moral or ideological grounds, the right of the Dáil to disestablish the Republic. Although some may have trusted Collins's assurances on the Boundary Commission, it is striking how rarely partition features. For Irish republicans, as for British politicians like Churchill, symbolic issues centring on sovereignty such as the oath of fealty, the status of the monarch, and membership of the British Empire, were paramount.

The historian Joe Lee has described the Treaty as the occasion rather than cause of the Civil War. The failure to achieve the Republic brought to a head longstanding tensions within a party which encompassed dual monarchists, pragmatic nationalists, and separatists opposed to any link with Britain. It ignited festering tensions between rival personalities, which became further entangled with issues of political principle. Although often framed as a conflict between supporters of the Republic and those who had abandoned it, the divisions that shaped the Civil War were more complex, with de Valera's proposed alternative to the Treaty repudiated by some anti-Treaty IRA leaders. The factors that determined the stance of ordinary IRA men, which included social and class divisions as well as local rivalries, were not restricted to attitudes to the Treaty.

How do these voices from history add to our understanding of the Irish revolution? Like all useful primary sources, they complicate the picture. One of the greatest impediments to understanding the past is our knowledge of what happened next. These accounts remind us how those who lived through this era acted in the expectation of different outcomes. Prior to the outbreak of the First World War, most Irish people – including republicans – anticipated a Home Rule parliament. The conflict that many feared in 1913 was not between separatists and the British authorities but between the Ulster Volunteer Force and the British army, or between Catholic nationalists and Protestant unionists in the North. Few expected a lengthy war when Redmond declared his support for Irish enlistment in the British army in September 1914.

The value of these texts does not lie solely in the factual light they shed on past events. Like all subjective sources, they are in some respects unreliable, reflecting bias, self-importance or other limitations. Most obviously, they reflect the times in which they were written; O'Hegarty's views on women, for example, have not aged well. As a result, they illuminate mentalities, as well as the memory of the revolution, a growing area of research. Mossie Harnett was one of several thousand veterans who felt compelled to record their experiences for posterity, many doing so in the 1940s and 1950s as they themselves began to pass into history. The realisation that patriots like Seán Connolly – ordinary people who achieved remarkable things – were no longer remembered outside their own townland prompted Ernie O'Malley to write his biographical account. He was also motivated by his concern, widely shared by veterans, that their sacrifices were no longer appreciated or even understood: 'Song and story that once stirred men no longer move a younger generation.' Hence, O'Malley's determination to record, not just Connolly's story, but that of hundreds of unknown soldiers in the final decades of his life, in the hope that their stories could be 'made into a patchwork quilt from memory'. This aim alone provides a compelling reason to ensure the wider availability of eye-witness accounts, particularly during a period of commemoration in which politicians and others will claim to speak on their behalf.

Greater familiarity with contemporary sources, such as the recently digitised witness statements of the Bureau of Military History, should complicate as well as inform commemoration. Although the idealism and achievements of the founding generation will rightly be honoured in 2016, the urge to celebrate independence should be tempered by an unsentimental understanding of the process by which it was achieved. P. S. O'Hegarty's belief that the violence of the revolution killed the spirit of the national movement was shared by many after the Civil War. Violence accelerated the pace of political change, resulting in a level of independence that few anticipated before 1914, but it also narrowed the space for an accommodation between Ireland's different traditions. Despite the relative success of the republican campaign, a significant moment in the global history of anti-imperialism, Irish revolutionaries did not achieve their central aims: the restoration of Gaelic, separation from England (for many, the essence of republicanism), and a united Ireland. Nor did they fully comprehend the contradictions between the last and first two of these aims. Independence, moreover, did not always live up to expectations, as the enthusiasm of the revival gave way to a conservative State. The revolution produced losers as well as winners, including minorities on both sides of the border. It is clear from the Military Service Pensions collection that many veterans endured hardship after, as well as during, the conflict. Few, though, regretted their efforts to achieve the republic of their dreams. Despite the political complexities of the period, and the limitations of their achievements, the revolutionary generation's refusal to bend the knee against more powerful forces will continue to inspire.

Fearghal McGarry is Reader in Irish History at the School of History and Anthropology at Queen's University Belfast. His most recent book is *The Abbey Rebels of Easter 1916: A Lost Revolution* (Dublin, 2015).

INTRODUCTION
Tom Garvin

P. S. O'Hegarty
Biographical Note

Patrick Sarsfield ("P. S.") O'Hegarty, Irish patriot, revolutionary, writer and civil servant, was born at Carrignavar, County Cork, in 1879. He had one brother, John (Jack, later Sean), born in 1881. His mother, Katherine Hallahan, came of west Cork farming stock, like Michael Collins. Two of her uncles had died in the great famine. His father, John Hegarty, a plaster and stucco worker, left Cork in the 1860s and later had his own business in Massachusetts. He was a member of the Fenian Brotherhood, as P.S. and Jack were also to be in their turn. The Hegartys returned to Ireland, where they set up in business, and prospered in a modest way until John's premature death forced the mother out to work.

P. S. was educated by the Christian Brothers at the "North Mon" in Cork city, was a law clerk for a while, and then entered the Post Office, again like Michael Collins. From his youth he was a voracious reader, and his range of acquaintance with English literature was formidable; his understanding of Irish literature was advanced and liberal, and arguably generations ahead of his time and of many of his comrades.

Subsequently he transferred to London, where he, like many young Irishmen who became politically conspicuous afterwards, worked in Mountpleasant Post Office. He was one of a group of young Irish civil servants living in London between 1902 and 1913 who were, collectively and individually, to become of major political significance. Many of them, like P. S., became members of the Irish Republican Brotherhood (IRB or Fenian Brotherhood). Many also played Gaelic games and participated in the Gaelic League's cultural activities. Michael Collins would have been one of the most conspicuous of the younger members of this group, and O'Hegarty knew him well, although P. S. was a decade older. As Secretary of the Central London Branch, Sinn Féin, P. S. had signed Michael's membership card. Padraig O Conaire, Robert Lynd and Bulmer Hobson were members of the circle as well, and P. S. retained lifelong friendships with Lynd and Hobson in particular.

He also knew Terence (Terry) MacSwiney well, as they had been schoolfellows in Cork. P. S. had a fairly intense correspondence with Terry while in London; in particular, the two young men argued by post about their attitude to the relationships that did, or should, exist between church and state in any society and, naturally, in Irish society in particular. Whereas P.S. and Collins joined the IRB, Terry refused to join, like the young Eamonn de Valera, as he respected the Catholic Church's prohibition on membership of secret, oath-sworn societies. In a kind of pre-enactment of Joyce's Shem the Penman and Shaun the Post, stay-at-home Terry and London-based P. S. argued politics, rather like bright young well-read people anywhere or anywhen. In 1904, for example, P.S. wrote to Terence ("Terry") in Cork

> I don't hold that the priests are our natural enemies but I do think strongly that they have acquired the habit and that nothing but strong determined actions will break them of it. They ruined every movement—directly or indirectly—since the passing of the Maynooth Grant in 1795 and we have to put them in their places if we are going to do anything . . . Most of the fellows here are anti-cleric to a greater or lesser degree . . . It is only when a man leaves Ireland that he begins to see straight on some things, this among them.

Later the same year he wrote to Terry, in response to some pieties transmitted to him from Cork by his friend,

> You appear to assume that anti-clericalism is atheism, which it is not. Anti-clericalism, as I look at it and as most fellows I know look at it, is simply anti-political-priestism . . . If you say a

word against the political priest, against any political action or
dogma of his, you are an atheist, a damned soul, you are
anathema, and you know that as well as I. You may do the
magnanimous and try to distinguish between the priest and
the Church *but he won't let you,* he deliberately and immorally
utilises his priestly influence to supplement the want of reason
in his argument.[1]

P. S. was particularly active in the London Gaelic League
and other Irish nationalist organisations of the time and
place, and was inducted into the IRB along with many other
enthusiastic young Irishmen of the time. He quickly became a
member of the Supreme Council of the IRB, dedicated as an
organisation to a "physical force" solution of the Irish Problem.
P.S. was himself a moderate and humane man, and was to
disagree with Collins as to the necessity of a military struggle
after the Easter, 1916 and Conscription, 1918, episodes. *The
Victory of Sinn Féin* deals with this at length.

In 1913, he was transferred back to his home town of
Cork, but was shifted back to England when the World War
broke out. In 1915, he married Wilhelmina Rebecca Smyth,
the daughter of a Presbyterian clergyman. His allegiance to the
seperatist cause and to Arthur Griffith's Sinn Féin forced him
to refuse an oath of allegiance to the British Crown in 1918,
when such an oath became obligatory. This obligation was
imposed, very foolishly, on rebel Irishmen by Dublin Castle.
British Ireland disintegrated in part because of this kind of
behaviour on the part of its rulers. P. S. set up the Irish
Bookshop in Dawson Street.

O'Hegarty took the pro-Treaty side after December, 1921
and wrote what was a brilliant polemic about the events of the
period, *The Victory of Sinn Féin,* published in Dublin in 1924
and, interestingly, never republished until now. He was a
prolific writer, and was an early contributor to the IRB journal,

[1]. Archives Department, University College, Dublin, MacSwiney
Papers, P48b/374–88. I am heavily indebted to Cian Ó hÉigeartaigh
for a copy of an essay on his grandfather published by him in *The
Irish Times* in 1979 (Typescript version in my possession, courtesy of
the author), and for subsequent correspondence and conversations.

Irish Freedom (1910–1914), a profoundly liberal and republican nationalist paper by the standards of the time. He tried valiantly to heal the Treaty division in 1922 by editing a short-lived journal, *The Separatist*. P. S. vehemently opposed any attempt to coerce the North into a united Ireland, enunciating a doctrine of Northern consent long before it was profitable or popular.

He was a prolific writer, and, besides *The Victory of Sinn Féin*, he wrote *A History of Ireland Under the Union* (1951). The latter book became a standard history of the period for about fifteen years and was, despite, or possibly because of, its argumentatively nationalistic thrust, well-regarded. Interestingly, its account of the events dealt with in *The Victory of Sinn Féin* rows back somewhat from that in the earlier book and is somewhat gentler on the anti-Treatyites, while retaining his central charge against Éamon de Valera, that he changed a difference of opinion into a split and sowed the seed of civil war.

Other works by O'Hegarty included assessments of John Mitchel and of his friend Terence Macswiney.

P.S. was, like so many of the London-Irish group of Irish revolutionaries, very much in favour of the revival of the Irish language. His family was reared Irish-speaking, and his son, Seán, founded the well-known Irish-language publishing house, Sairséal agus Dill (the names are derived from the two sides of his parental ancestry, and apparently also symbolise alliances between the North and South and between Catholic and Protestant). However, he was no literary bigot; he denounced Daniel Corkery's narrow and provincial definition of Irish literature, immediately recognised Joyce's *Ulysses* as a masterpiece, and saluted O'Casey's *The Plough and the Stars* in the face of howls of nationalist and clerical denunciation.

He was Secretary of the Department of Posts and Telegraphs from 1922 to his retirement date of 1944. He died in 1955. He was a true Fenian.

The Victory of Sinn Féin

The Victory of Sinn Féin is one of a select group of extended
memoirs written by someone who was close to the centre of
things in Irish separatist politics during the most crucial phase
of the movement. Comparison might be drawn with such
classics as C. S. Andrews's *Dublin Made Me* or Ernie O'Malley's
On Another Man's Wound. However, the two latter works are
written from a pronouncedly republican point of view, and
have remained rather better known. The O'Malley book is
less reliable than the O'Hegarty book as a memoir written in
the immediacy of the events, as it was written much later and
strives towards literary effect rather than towards strict historical
accuracy. Andrews was trying to give an accurate and con-
scientious account of what happened as he remembered it,
and of his own state of mind as a young IRA volunteer.
However, he wrote a generation after the events. A comparison
might be drawn also with Ernest Blythe's Irish-language trilogy,
which would merit translation and a wider readership.

O'Hegarty's book is written from a political point of view
that has been almost forgotten. The clearest statement of it
that I have come across other than *Victory* is Eimear O'Duffy's
fictional *The Wasted Island*. Both argue passionately that most
of the violence associated with the independence movement
was unnecessary and even self-defeating. O'Hegarty regretfully
accepted the inevitability of a defensive "War of Independence",
but argued that violence had no further role to play after the
Truce of July 1921. He argued also that the Rising of 1916
was sufficient; a protest in arms had been made, and the rest
should have been left to political negotiation.

Whatever about the Anglo-Irish War, the Irish Civil War,
he argued, was an avoidable disaster, one which killed the
spirit of the national movement. His heroes were Arthur
Griffith and Michael Collins; to him, Griffith was the wise
leader, always in the background, always trying to subordinate
military considerations to the political purposes which he saw
as being far more important. At one stage (May, 1920), when
the IRA proposed some unnamed enormity, he said to P. S.

> The military mind is the same in every country. Our military
> men are as bad as the British. They think of nothing but their
> own particular end, and cannot be brought to consider the
> political consequences of their proceedings.

Griffith is portrayed as being free of obsession about symbolic forms, and wanting Irish independence, under even the Hanoverian crown if necessary. Arguments about Free State versus Republic were, to him, pointless. What counted were the means of state power: control of the army, of taxation and of customs. Given those, all else would follow. P. S. was substantially in sympathy with this point of view. Unfortunately, not all the leaders saw it that way.

The character sketches of Griffith, Collins and de Valera are vivid, and make one feel almost as if one had met them and been on close terms with them. Even now, the treatment of de Valera may give offence, much as did Neil Jordan's treatment of him in the *Michael Collins* film of 1996. However, many people, at the end of the century, see de Valera from a very different standpoint. Two generations later, de Valera is remembered by many as a statesman, a wise and wily politician who legitimated the state, built up national morale in the 1930s, ensured that the country would weather the Second World War and, perhaps, outstayed his welcome in power in the 1950s. His behaviour in 1921–23 has been forgotten or forgiven, perhaps wrongly, perhaps wisely.

Certainly, de Valera's extraordinary conduct in 1922 when he permitted his name to be associated with a ghost presidency of a ghost republic under the actual control of Liam Lynch's rump IRA did untold damage to an emergent Irish political culture. It permitted many to question the constitutional continuity from Griffith's Dáil government to Cosgrave's Free State and it provided alibis for murder afterwards. Whether de Valera knew what he was doing is another question; I have argued elsewhere that he was still learning his job as a political leader and did not learn quickly enough. He was also extraordinarily self-righteous, untrusting and unwilling to have his equals in ability close to his throne. He came to fear and even hate Collins and Griffith, seeing them as betrayers of *him,* never mind Ireland. My suspicion is that his own actions led him to suffer a nervous breakdown in 1922 and he would, in the eyes of a later generation, be regarded as seriously ill during the period and not fully responsible for his actions. Certainly, de Valera can be accused, at the very least, of creating a culture of complaint and denial, and of infantilising much Irish political discourse subsequently. O'Hegarty takes a less kind view.

The Victory of Sinn Féin is very much a polemic and a period piece, as the author himself willingly admits. The affectionate portrait of Collins is familiar, and does not differ much from other sketches of the man; it is evident that P. S. knew Collins best of the three main dramatis personae in his book. The hero-worship of Griffith, the demonisation of de Valera, the less than sentimental treatment of the women activists will strike some minds as extreme and possibly offensive. However, his point of view was not eccentric or outlandish at that time; much of what O'Hegarty says would have been accepted by very many people of his generation.[1] For this reason alone, it is a valuable source for IRB and "Free State" mentality and gives a view of the period of Irish history which the author lived through that is invaluable, illuminating and, possibly, surprising. It was written in a hurry, and is sometimes repetitive; however, it is also written with enormous passion, verve and energy; it reads like a thriller.

[1.] For similar contemporary views on the republican women, Archives Department, University College Dublin, Batt O'Connor Papers, P68, 28 December, 1921; Michael Hayes Papers, P53/303; *Freeman's Journal*, 21, 23 February 1922. Cf. my treatment of the anti-treatyites in my *1922: the Birth of Irish Democracy*, Dublin: 1996, 97–104.

P. S. O'Hegarty in his Library *c.* 1952
(photograph by Seán Ó hEigeartaigh)

TO
MY GRANDCHILDREN

NOTE ON THE TEXT

The text of this edition is that of the original book published in Dublin by the Talbot Press in 1924. It is complete and the author's own punctuation and corrections (on page 164) are retained.

PREFACE

This book is not a history. The true history of a passionate period such as that dealt with cannot be written by any contemporary. We are all too near it. Nor can anybody who has lived through the Split and the Irregular War ever really look at them with that fair-mindedness which the historian must exercise.

It will be at least a generation before the factors that admit the writing of a real history can be present—the fair-mindedness and all the necessary documents and data. The only thing a contemporary can do is to record such material as he can as may help a future historian.

What this book is, then, is a book recording the impressions which the whole thing has made upon a contemporary who has worked hard for Ireland, whose hobby has always been the study of history, and who has thereby been accustomed to estimate forces and tendencies and to attempt to relate Irish happenings to the general principles behind them.

In compiling the book, I have not used the Treaty Debates nor any of the documents about a particular event issued after the event. I have put down events exactly as it seemed to me they happened; and I have drawn such conclusions from known facts as the information in my possession seemed to warrant. The conversations which I report are reported in their exact words. I did not note them down at the time, but I knew their importance and I memorised them carefully. I happen to have a good memory.

The book will be deeply, and perhaps deservedly, unpopular. I have had to say things about the Movement, both before the Truce and after the Truce, which will not be relished. I have had to write hard things about some of my friends directly, and even harder things about others by implication. But what I have written I have written because I believe it to be the truth, and because the Cause we all—those who shot Mick Collins and those who shot Cathal Brugha alike—stand for ultimately can be helped only by truth and honesty.

I have said nothing about the Six-County question in the book, because the boundary position, as I write, is at a stage at which writing can do no good. But the essential facts about Ulster are given in my 1919 pamphlet *(Ulster: A Brief Statement of Fact),* and they cannot be altered by any transient English juggling with Ulster territory, or by any muddling which any particular Irish generation may accomplish.

P. S. O'Hegarty   *December,* 1924.

THE VICTORY OF SINN FÉIN

HOW IT WON IT AND HOW IT USED IT

CHAPTER 1.

THE INSURRECTION OF 1916.

At the outbreak of the European War the Irish people were swept off their feet by the wave of British propaganda which was directed against them, powerfully aided by Press and Parliamentary Party. They became anti-German and pro-British. The minority of separatists who tried to keep Ireland clear of the conflict, who saw in the war Ireland's great opportunity to play for her own freedom, was almost snowed under. But that pro-British sentiment in the Irish people was passive rather than active. Although they felt that England was right in the war, they did not feel that they were called upon to do anything in the way of helping England otherwise than by feeding her; and when it began to be plain that England was presuming on Irish sympathy to coquet with the idea of Irish conscription, a reaction, helped also by the coercive measures employed against the Irish Volunteers, set in.

But it was only a very slight reaction. The Irish Volunteers increased in strength, but they had no support, and they served only to draw attention to the fact that the mass of the people remained pro-British. Ireland had suspended its Home Rule Bill, suspended its claim until the end of the war, and it went its way placidly, seeing itself England's chief source of cattle and dairy produce until the end of the war, when a grateful England would present Ireland with a Home Rule Bill.

But the war had changed the whole alignment of political forces, and underneath its surface placidity Ireland was seething. The war, which had solved for the British the question of the Home Rule Bill, had solved something also for the Irish

Republican Brotherhood. It had freed it from the Fabian policy which for years it had adopted, and given it the opportunity and the right to strike. While people and parties looked at each other bewildered, and heaved sighs of relief at the postponement of awkwardnesses, the I.R.B. acted. In August, 1914, a meeting of its Supreme Council was held at which the decision was taken to make an insurrection before the end of the war; and upon that all its energies were bent. That was the origin of the Insurrection of 1916, that and not the Dublin strike, nor the Citizen Army, nor any other of the reasons which have been given. The Insurrection of 1916 came because the Supreme Council of the Irish Republican Brotherhood decided that it would come, decided that Ireland's honour would be tarnished if the war were to be allowed to pass, as the Boer War had been, without a fight being made. And it was the Supreme Council of the I.R.B. which decided the Insurrection, planned it, organised it, led it, and financed it. Had it not been for it, there would have been no insurrection. Of the seven men who signed the Proclamation six were I.R.B. men. The seventh, James Connolly, though not an I.R.B. man, had been working with them for some time beforehand, in what might be termed "external association."

The insurrection came upon the people of Ireland like a thunderbolt. They had not been expecting it, and they did not want it. Although the effect of British propaganda was weakening, and there was a certain reaction in favour of complete Irish neutrality, yet the great mass of the people still hazily believed in the Allies and did not want England embarrassed. The insurrection was therefore universally and explosively unpopular. The populace fraternised with the British soldiery during the fighting, gave them food and smiles: in Cork, the Redmondite Volunteers mobilised and helped the British by guarding bridges, etc.; in Dublin, the populace attacked the wives of the men who were fighting; and the resolutions of various public bodies in the country condemning the insurrection may still be read. If Ireland as a whole could have got hold of Tom Clarke and his comrades during that week it would have torn them to pieces.

For a moment the whole fate of Ireland stood in the balance. Had the English but the wit to see it, the insurrection played right into their hands. If it had come with the Volunteers unanimously behind it, it would have still played into their hands, but coming as it did with the Volunteers divided between those who went out and those who did not go out, coming as the culmination of the policy of a minority using the organisation of the Volunteers without the knowledge of the executive of that body, the field for English exploitation was tremendous. If they had laughed at it, tried the promoters before a magistrate and ridiculed the whole thing, with no general arrests and no long vindictive sentences, they could have done what they liked with Ireland. But the completeness of their victory, their crushing of the insurrection with the approval of the Irish Parliamentary Party and of the mass of Irish public opinion, took away their political sanity. The army and the *Irish Times* demanded blood, and blood they got. But when Sir John Maxwell shot to pieces the Government of the Irish Republic he put an end to the English domination of Ireland.

The insurrection of 1916 was a forlorn hope and a deliberate blood sacrifice. The men who planned it and led it did not expect to win. They knew they could not win. They knew that the people were against them and that the people would hate them for it. But they counted upon being executed afterwards and they knew that *that* would save Ireland's soul. The European war had shown Ireland to be less Irish and more Anglicised than ever she had been in her history, had shown Ireland to be more than three-fourths assimilated to England; and they offered up their lives as a sacrifice to recall the nation to heroic thoughts and heroic deeds, to remind the people that they were a *nation* and not a dependency. Never did any body or men go forth on a more desperate enterprise, with purer heads, or more unfaltering courage. They played for the soul of Ireland, and they knew that it was a sheer gamble.

But when Tom Clarke faced the firing squad in Kilmainham, he knew that he had won, and that the soul of Ireland would go back to the old heroic thoughts and heroic ways. Those May morning volleys blotted out the old Ireland.

CHAPTER II.

THE RE-EMERGENCE OF SINN FÉIN.

The effect of the executions in Ireland was not immediately apparent. The people were bewildered and cowed, and were still suffering from the effects of their year-and-a-half's pro-English bath. The first voice to be raised in favour of the insurrection was that of Mr. Shaw, whose fine letter in the *Daily News* of the 10th May, 1916, places him definitely among the separatists; and the next was that of Dr. O'Dwyer, the Bishop of Limerick. Then came other voices. Mr. William O'Brien, whose fundamental nationalism is stronger than his factionism, threw his paper practically on the side of the insurrection; and even Mr. John Dillon was stirred into rediscovering his nationalism, and made a speech in the British Parliament which was almost a separatist one. Slowly, but with increasing speed, the tide set in against England, against the Irish Parliamentary Party and the whole policy it stood for, and in favour of the thing for which the insurrection had been made. This new political wave had as yet no leader, and no policy; but it had a battle cry *"Up the Rebels!"* and that sufficed. With that cry in its ears, Ireland turned and gave heed to the dead.

The Sinn Féin organisation, from being a serious threat to the Irish Parliamentary Party in 1907, had dwindled away until, at the time of the insurrection, it was practically confined to one central branch in Dublin; while it survived as a political policy through Mr. Griffith's paper, *Nationality*. But it seemed to have become so harmless that when the orators and the Press of the Irish Party wanted to discredit the Irish Volunteers in 1914, they called them the *Sinn Féin* Volunteers. And now, with a similar motive, they called the insurrection the *Sinn Féin* Insurrection. Ireland then knew nothing of the I.R.B. It knew that it was the Volunteers who had insurrected, and as it began to turn towards that insurrection, it began to examine those who made it. It was told that they were *Sinn Féiners*, and it was told that the insurrection was a Sinn Féin insurrection. So that it began to ask questions about Sinn Féin, about what it was and who it was, and what its policy was.

The British had shot or imprisoned the leaders of the insurrection. They had, in addition, interned every man in Ireland who was known to have been connected with the Volunteers or Sinn Féin. Mr. Griffith, who *was* Sinn Féin, they had interned under instructions from the *Irish Times*. And therefore the popular demand for information about Sinn Féin was not very completely met. But pamphlets began to appear, and leaflets, and ballads, and weekly papers; the I.R.B. was going again and working at a rebinding of the threads; and such of the Volunteers as had escaped the net were drawn together and formed a nucleus for the re-establishment of that organisation. So that, gradually, all the impulses working in Ireland against England coalesced in a vague mass of unorganised emotion, which was Sinn Féin without knowing what that was, which felt instinctively that Sinn Féin held within it that public policy which it was looking for, and which, while waiting for a lead on Sinn Féin, shouted "Up the Rebels!" bought ballads and mosquito papers, and hoped. The Sinn Féin movement, in fact, in the form in which Griffith always wanted it, was being created. While Mr. H. M. Pim, in his paper *The Irishman,* kept the name of Griffith prominently before his readers, assuring them, in every issue, that they need not worry about policy, that Arthur Griffith would give them that when he got out of prison, that he *would* get out of prison, and that until he did get out they should wait and be ready to follow him.

All this had its effect. As Ireland became pro-insurrection she became Sinn Féin, without knowing what Sinn Féin was, except that it stood generally for Irish independence in the old complete way, the way in which the Irish Party had not stood for it. On the other hand there was no Sinn Féin organisation, and in so far as the new wave was getting itself organised at all, it was getting itself organised—the revolutionary section of it—in the I.R.B. and Irish Volunteers. There were practically two sides to the movement, a great public emotional wave towards the insurrection which had seized upon Sinn Féin as one concrete thing in the welter which it was faced with, and a secret organisation, in their old organisations, of the remnants of the I.R.B. and the Volunteers, with such new revolutionary recruits as they had been able to secure.

While this had been going on in Ireland, something similar, but more conscious and binding, had been going on in the prisons and in the internment camps. Many a Sinn Féin branch which had been moribund for years found itself together again in a prison or camp. Conversations, interchange of views, interchange of plans, were not uncommon in the prisons, but in the camps they were the order of the day. Some got their education in Sinn Féin principles, some in I.R.B. principles, some in Gaelic League principles, but all got something, and a mass which went to prison and camp all sorts and conditions of men, was welded in these educational institutions into a loose but genuine whole. And therefore when the internment camps opened their doors at Christmas, 1916, for all the untried prisoners not considered to be dangerous, the new Irish movement was at once supplied with leaders who knew each other's minds, who knew what they wanted to do and how they meant to do it. The men who came out took control both of the Irish Volunteers and of the I.R.B., and they set about organising the vague Sinn Féin feelings of the country into a real and vital public organisation. The whole movement was co-ordinated and tightened, and with Griffith a free man, and the publication of *Nationality*, the people got both men and policy. Griffith had preached for years, patiently and doggedly, to a handful. Now he preached to a nation, which listened as to a gospel. The result was a comprehensive national movement which combined the revolutionary emotion of the aftermath of the insurrection with the clear intellectuality of Sinn Féin—a Revolutionary Movement which had a revolutionary aim and an evolutionary method.

Previous Irish insurrections, after physical failure, had ended in reactions which buried them, because they had only one weapon, because they had no public policy, no civilian evolutionary policy to fall back upon when the revolutionary policy failed them. The insurrection of 1916 had the policy of Sinn Féin to fall back upon—and the man of that policy; and to that policy it attracted in time the mass of the Irish people, which it could not have done on a purely revolutionary policy. Griffith had always known that the policy of Parliamentarianism would fail Ireland in his life-time, and that that failure would be apparent to the Irish people. He had always known also that, apart from physical force, Ireland could win her a freedom by moral force and passive resistance and an intensive constructive policy, as outlined in Sinn Féin; and therefore he had been content to go on working and preaching, in poverty and in neglect, so long as he maintained his policy ready for the nation. And in Ireland's hour of need the policy was there ready, and the man. Sinn Féin re-emerged, dominating Ireland as completely as the Parliamentarian policy had in its greatest strength.

CHAPTER III.

THE IRISH REPUBLICAN BROTHERHOOD.

Ever since its foundation in 1858, the Irish Republican Brotherhood had been the only stable political force in Ireland, and to it Ireland owes it that in every generation there was a continuing separatist tradition. The I.R.B. was often weak, it was often split, but it was always there, watching out for any chance which might present itself for forwarding separatist principles. Its function has been the function of a watchdog, and steadfastly and faithfully it fulfilled that function over sixty years. It watched everything in Ireland, it was in everything, and whenever there was an opportunity, however small, of doing anything to forward the separatist cause, the I.R.B. was there to do it.

In the past three years the I.R.B. has been in the mouths of many people who never were members of it, who never would be members of it, and who until quite recently attacked it and the things for which it stood. It has been in the mouths of many others who had never even heard of it until they began to abuse it. None of these people know anything about it, about its organisation or its aims or its work. None of these people know anything about the way in which the movement they have ruined was made, about the hard, unpaid, untrumpeted work of common unpretentious men of all ages in the years between the rise of Parnell and the Election of 1918. Revolutionary movements do not rise up from the ground in a night, or in a year, or in ten years. The seed has to be sown over a long series of years, and men have to die and to be broken, to go hungry and jobless, so that the principle may live. The Separatist movement of 1918 was the result of seed sown by the I.R.B. and the *Gaelic League* and the *United Irishman*; but the I.R.B. was the parent and the watcher. It helped and guided the others, it co-ordinated and organised, and at the supreme moment it acted. In the twenty years preceding 1916 it was but a minority of a minority. Its whole membership could have been comprised in a concert hall. But it was a membership of convinced and unpaid separatists, and it included some of the best brains in Ireland. It had members everywhere, its tentacles went into everything, it maintained a footing in every organisation and movement in Ireland which could be supported without doing violence to separatist principles. Everywhere it pushed separatist principles. And when money was needed at a pinch for any of the organisations which it regarded as key organisations—the Gaelic League, Sinn Féin, the Gaelic Athletic Association, the Fianna, and the Irish Volunteers—it found the money. Strange and transient Committees and Societies were constantly cropping up, doing this and that specific national work. The I.R.B. formed them. The I.R.B. ran them. The I.R.B. provided the money. The I.R.B. dissolved them when their work was done. The major portion of its funds, without which the home organisation would have been helpless because of its paucity of numbers and the poverty of its members, came from the Clan na Gael of America, which played the same part in American-Irish organisations that the I.R.B. played at home, and to which no appeal for money for an object even remotely separatist was ever made in vain.

In this matter I am writing of what I know. I became a member of the I.R.B. in 1903. From 1908 until my deportation in August, 1914, I was a member of its Supreme Council. The policy outlined above was the policy we inherited from our predecessors, the policy which we in our turn adopted and pushed, and, I think, made thoroughly effective. We kept the whole of Ireland and every happening, and every possible happening, constantly under view, and we threw our weight wherever it seemed to us that we could best advantage the cause. That was how the Irish Volunteers came to be started.

Before ever there had been so much as a public whisper of a Volunteer force, the Council had discussed it. It decided that any such force started by physical-force-men or by advanced nationalists would be suppressed, but it felt also that the Ulster force made it difficult to suppress a Southern force which would be sponsored by unsuspectable people. And that was how Eoin MacNeill and Larry Kettle and other unsuspectable people started the Irish Volunteers. They thought they were acting on impulse when they were really acting on suggestion. Everything they did, then and afterwards, was supervised. Tom Clarke, standing behind his counter on the night the Irish Volunteers were launched, could smile and go home happy. The cheers, the overflow meetings, the non-suppression, were meat and drink to him. He had been one of the strongest of us in wishing that no desire on our part to get in on the movement should be allowed to jeopardise it.

The war changed all that. A meeting of the Council, held in August, 1914, to discuss the new situation, decided that this was Ireland's opportunity, and that an insurrection should be prepared for and should be launched before the end of the war. And Mr. Redmond's attempt to turn the Volunteers into British soldiers ended that movement as an All-Ireland one. It fell naturally into I.R.B. hands. There has been much talk, and much writing, as to who was responsible for the insurrection, and I doubt if Mr. Robert Lynd's sentimental attribution of it to the Dublin Strike and the Citizen Army and James Connolly will ever be overtaken. But the insurrection came because the Supreme Council of the I.R.B. decided on an insurrection. They financed it. They used in its furtherance the organisation of the Irish Volunteers without the knowledge of the Volunteers' Executive. They were a movement within movements. They decided its date, and its manner. And when the insurrection did come, the Proclamation of the Irish Republic was signed by six members of the I.R.B. and one Socialist-Republican who, though actually not a member, had worked in close touch with the organisation for months beforehand.

In May, 1915, Seán MacDermott called to see me at Welshpool, and gave me a full account of the position. He told me that they were preparing an insurrection, that they had established at the beginning a Military Council to work out plans, that at the first meeting of that Council Joe Plunkett produced complete plans for a Dublin insurrection, on which it appeared he had been working for years, and that these had been adopted practically in their entirety. He told me the plan, and it was identical, even to the names of the buildings occupied, with what actually happened. He told me also that they were negotiating for German assistance, but would go on in any case, and that they contemplated a Dublin insurrection only, an insurrection which would make its protest, in the name of the Historic Irish Nation, against the Redmond slavishness, and would re-assert Ireland's claim to independence. He said: "We'll hold Dublin for a week, but we'll save Ireland." He used strong language about Connolly, said they had had a lot of trouble with him and expected more, and that unless they could bring him to reason they were afraid that he would say or do something which would put the British on the alert. That culminated afterwards in the kidnapping of Connolly and his detention for several days, until he had agreed to fall in with the I.R.B. plans and arrangements.

At any rate, whether Ireland of the coming times gives the insurrection praise or blame, it will place the responsibility for it where it is due, on the I.R.B. It was due to it, to the teaching and the planning of the young men who controlled it from 1909, and who wrote *Irish Freedom* (1911–1914), that a physical force separatist wind blew again in Ireland. It was due to it that when another war came the Prime Minister of England was unable to taunt Ireland as Salisbury had taunted the Irish Parliamentary Party after the Boer War, when he said that he had been able, during that war, to remove every able-bodied British soldier from Ireland and hold the country by a handful of cripples. It was due to it that the British soldiers were removed, able-bodied and crippled alike, never again to come back.

CHAPTER IV.

DE VALERA.

Prior to the Insurrection of 1916, Mr. de Valera was unknown in Ireland, outside Gaelic League and Volunteer circles in Dublin, and there he was not a leader, nor did he aspire to be. He had no political ambitions, and refused nomination for the Executive of the Volunteers because he did not want to touch the political end of the movement. He was opposed to the insurrection, as most people were, but when the final orders came he obeyed orders and fought through the whole week. He was the last Commandant to surrender, and the only one to escape execution.

When the people, after the Rising, having dwelt sufficiently on the dead leaders, began to consider the living, they dwelt naturally on de Valera. Everything combined to make them do so. He was the senior officer of the Volunteers left, and he was as a man preserved by special providence for something to come. The circumstances of his surrender, something heroic and noble in his behaviour, had marked him out and had focussed public attention on him. In the prison in which he and others were confined he was placed, by general agreement, in command of the prisoners, and it is told of him that, meeting one day Eoin MacNeill on the stairs of the prison, he gave him the salute to which, as Chief of Staff of the Volunteers, he was entitled, and made the other men also give it, thus acting in the spirit of the message of Pearse's in which he said: "Both MacNeill and we have done what we thought best for Ireland." In prison he thought and grew, feeling the responsibility of leadership, feeling, doubtless, that there was left to him particularly a charge and a legacy from the Dead. And when the prison doors were opened in 1917, de Valera came home as the leader of the returning prisoners and, therefore, the embodiment in the public mind of the insurrection and all that it stood for.

In the meantime, events in the country had been moving. "Up the Rebels!" had won bye-elections at North Roscommon and South Longford; and while the latter was won by only thirty-seven votes, it was won after a campaign during which each side put forth its full strength, and it was therefore regarded as decisive. It showed that the country had definitely swung against the policy of the Irish Parliamentary Party, for South Longford had been regarded as a safe and conservative constituency. Then came a vacancy in East Clare, caused by the death of William Redmond in France, and Mr. de Valera was nominated for it. At this time the Government decided to release the remainder of the prisoners, the men who had been considered too dangerous to release at Christmas, 1916, in order to "create an atmosphere" for the Irish Convention, and accordingly de Valera, Griffith, MacNeill, and their comrades came home in June, 1917, to find a whole people welcoming them and acclaiming them. The scenes of wild enthusiasm which greeted them was the first indication many of them had that they were coming back to a changed Ireland. Well, they obliged Mr. Lloyd George; they created an atmosphere for the Convention. After a day or two in Dublin, during which Mr. de Valera announced that he stood by the Republican Proclamation, and quelled an attempt to down MacNeill by refusing to go on a platform in Clare without him, the whole selection moved down to Clare, and within a week Griffith reappeared with *Nationality*. The movement which had been growing was provided with its leaders.

In Clare, Mr. de Valera swept everything before him. His flight from an English prison fight down to Clare, had in it everything dramatic and emotional which counted; and the campaign, a soft of massed attack, with bands, flags, and uniforms, put him at the head of the poll by an unprecedented majority, and ended the sway of the Irish Parliamentary

Party. He returned to Dublin with all the *eclat* of victory, with all the enthusiasm and emotion which had been aroused by the insurrection centred on him, and at the Convention of Sinn Féin which was held immediately afterwards, he was elected President in succession to Griffith, who withdrew his own nomination, and himself proposed de Valera. De Valera's election was in a sense imposed on the Convention by the general feeling of the country, but also by the fact that he was the only leader whose leadership made unity possible. The two sides of the movement, the evolutionary Sinn Féin side and the revolutionary Easter Week side, had not then coalesced; and while the one would not touch MaeNeill or Griffith, the other would not touch Count Plunkett or Cathal Brugha. De Valera was acceptable to all.

And so began a curious situation. Mr. de Valera was leader, with all the public deference and consideration which his position carried with it. He was the voice of the movement, its public standard-bearer, its maker of pronouncements. But Griffith was still its brain-carrier and its supplier of ideas, and upon Griffith it was that the majority counted and depended. Mr. de Valera's nationalistic education was not, so to put it, completed. All the time between his election as leader in June, 1917, and his departure for America in June, 1919, he was learning, ploughing his way to knowledge through platitudes. In those pre-American days of his he was a slow-moving, painfully uncouth, massive, speaker, with a disarming habit of pouring forth as new discoveries things which had been for twenty years the commonplaces of separatist thought. His great value to the country was his honesty and his simplicity and his singlemindedness. He re-stated, in plain, simple language, in speeches which were of general application to the nations as well as of particular application to Ireland, the unassailable moral and international principles upon which Ireland's case rested. While his personality and his integrity had a big influence at home in ranging all sections of nationalist opinion behind the movement of which he was the spokesman.

CHAPTER V.

MICK COLLINS.

In the last years of his life, Mick Collins became almost a legendary character. The things attributed to him were so varied and so heroic that they might easily be legends about a mythical hero. Since his death, much legend has accumulated around his name, and I daresay more will accumulate. In this chapter I want to write the truth about him as I knew him.

It is not true, in the first place, that Mick Collins was a leader of the Irish in London. Everybody in Sinn Féin circles knew him, and everybody liked him, but he was not a leader. He had strong individuality, clearly-held opinions, and noticeable maturity even as a boy of seventeen, which was his age when he made his appearance in Irish circles in London. But his place there was rather as the raw material of a leader than as a leader. When he came to London as a mere boy, he fell into spasmodic association with a hard-drinking, hard-living crowd from his own place, and their influence on him was not good. During most of his years in London he was in the "blast and bloody" stage of adolescent evolution, and was regarded as a wild youth, with plenty of ability, who was spoiled by his wildness. Not that that wildness was any deeper than the surface. Behind it his mind grew and his ideas enlarged. But there was very little in the Mick Collins of those days to give promise of the man who was to come. Of his activities there, the only thing that need be said is that he was always on the right side in the many battles, on many different platforms, which Sinn Féin fought in its own organisation, in the Gaelic League, in the Gaelic Athletic Association, and finally in the

Irish Volunteers. And, to those who knew him then, those aspects of him will outlast all the pomp and glory of his years in Ireland. I, at any rate, find him coming to my memory far oftener in the semblance of the last hurling match we played together, than in the semblance of any later association.

It was the Editor of the *Irish Times*, I think (it could only be he), who, on his death, made some reference to his "want of education." It is true that he had had to earn his own living at an early age, and that he never attended a University. If attendance at a University constitutes education, then he certainly was not educated. But it does not, and Mick Collins was educated in the best of all schools, in the world of his own thought and his own experience. He was well-read in modern literature and drama and keen to talk about them, and in the great years of the Court Theatre, and in the weeks when the Manchester Repertory Company came to the Coronet, you would find him constantly in the gallery. He was growing and deepening in these years, growing in body and in mind, and reaching out, as a good mind does in adolescence and early manhood, towards every quickening and ennobling thing in life.

But it was Ireland that made a man of him, and Easter Week that threw him up, as it did De Valera. In January, 1916, he came to Dublin, with other London-Irish boys, and threw himself into the Volunteer movement. He fought in Easter Week, and went to Frongoch with the rest, where his energy, courage, and capacity for leadership asserted themselves. When the general release came, he threw himself into the movement with renewed zest. Mrs. Clarke, who had carried on the I.R.B. since Easter Week, now handed it over to the released men, and by his character and force Collins dominated it, as he did the Irish Volunteers. He was not yet a political force, but the German Plot made him that. When the Plot swept away the Standing Committee of Sinn Féin, Collins was the strongest personality and the ablest man on the reconstructed Executive. So that all the strings of the Irish movement—I.R.B., Volunteers, and Sinn Féin—were gathered together in one hand, and the whole movement was run as one movement by one brain acting through many men and in many ways. His ascendency was a clear ascendency of personal character, energy and ability. No work was too arduous or dangerous for him to undertake, no pains too great, nothing was too small for him to neglect it. When he made an appointment, he kept it punctually; and when he made a promise, he kept it punctiliously. He worked from nine in the morning until eleven, twelve, and later at night, and he watched and co-ordinated everything. He answered all letters, and promptly. And even in the darkest period of the war, he would go out of his way and take personal risks in order to help anybody, even people who were no more than acquaintances. He kept an eye upon every little detail in connection with his work, and he *knew* everybody who was entrusted with even the most perfunctory of tasks in connexion with any of his schemes. It was he who planned de Valera's escape from Lincoln, and he and Harry Boland who carried it out.

So it was that while the German Plot might have blunted the movement, it really had the effect of solidifying it. Father Michael O'Flanagan, to whose work at this period too much praise cannot be given, solidified it publicly, and Collins solidified its hidden sources. It was at this time that the movement as a whole became aware of him, sensed his personality and his leadership, began to love him and to have that trust in him which hitherto they had had in Griffith and de Valera. And so, when the prisoners came out after the failure of the Plot, they found a new leader. They found Collins doing everything, and leading everything, and trusted by everybody. He had won his place. And they accepted him. The wild youth had sown his wild oats, and had come into his manhood. It was a case of a man rising to his opportunities, and when the big call came to Collins, nobly he rose to it. He was now in his full manhood, a man with a big frame and a big heart, with a good face and chin, and with the friendliest and most winning smile that ever human being had. He had put all unworthiness behind him, and girt himself for this fight as became Ireland's spearpoint. None knew better than he how much depended on him, how much depended on his brain remaining clear and on all his faculties keeping alert. And from that to the end he was a Bayard, *sans peur et sans reproche,* sinking every personal thing in the cause of Ireland. He was no plaster saint. He did not go to Mass every morning. He retained to the end the habit of sometimes losing his temper and reverting to the blast and bloody speech of his adolescence. But he was a *Man,* and a clean, loveable one. He passed the great test for any adult, in that children loved him. Our little boy at the time (1918–19) that Mick stayed with us was between one-and-a-half and two years of age. He was extremely shy and normally cried when any stranger came to the house. The first time he saw Mick he went to him, sat on his knee, and played with him. I do not think Mick ever went to a house where there were children without becoming one of them. No man can get a finer certificate of character than that. "Suffer little children to come unto me." They came to Mick.

CHAPTER VI.

DAIL ÉIREANN.

The North Roscommon election in 1917, although it resulted in a heavy defeat for the Irish Parliamentary Party, was not taken too seriously by that party. They regarded it as a surprise result, a result to be attributed rather to emotion than to conviction. And when the next vacancy occurred, that at South Longford a few months later, they faced it in full confidence and with a machine in full working order. That was one of the vital elections in Irish history. If the Parliamentarians had won it, they might have preserved their organisation and their machine and kept Sinn Féin out of its heritage for some time yet; but they lost it by thirty-seven votes, and got their death-blow. It is true that, after that, they won Waterford and South Armagh bye-elections; but even they themselves recognised that these two had special circumstances which prevented either from having any general significance; and despite these two victories their organisation faded and their party dwindled and their confidence vanished. The professional politicians everywhere felt that the ship was sinking, and they deserted it and came over in masses to Sinn Féin. East Cavan, the last bye-election before the end of the war, returned Arthur Griffith by a huge majority; and in the few months following, the Sinn Féin organisation replaced that which for so many years had held Ireland for the Irish Parliamentary Party. At the General Election at Christmas, 1918, the Parliamentary Party contested only a proportion of the seats, were heavily defeated, and out of 106 members for the whole of Ireland, Sinn Féin elected 73. It had its mandate for Irish independence and for demanding the admission of Ireland to the Peace Conference at Versailles.

We did not realise it at the time, but what had happened was not that Sinn Féin had captured Ireland, but that the politicians in Ireland and those who make them, all the elements which had sniffed at Sinn Féin and libelled it, which had upheld corruption and jobbery, had realised that Sinn Féin was going to win, and had come over to it *en masse*. They gave their votes and their support to a programme, every item of which was anathema to them; but in their hearts they remained still corrupt, still just politicians. Everything played into Sinn Féin's hands. A policy of Birrellism might have held Ireland still for England, but instead we were given the mailed fist. The German Plot, Partition, Conscription—everything combined to throw more and more elements in the country over to Sinn Féin. The Labour Party gave it a free hand; and finally, its bitterest opponent, the Irish Hierarchy, came over to it and practically gave it their blessing. No such unity and no such enthusiasm had been seen in Ireland since the early Parnell days.

To those of us who had been in Sinn Féin from the beginning, it was difficult to realise that the Election of 1918 was not a dream. It went beyond the wildest dreams even the most sanguine of us had ever had. We knew what we were up against, and we had had no illusions as to the magnitude of the task we had set our hands to. We knew also that the policy of the Irish Parliamentary Party could not succeed, and that when its failure became apparent to Ireland she would fall back upon our policy or some modification of it. But that in our lifetime we would see the whole of Ireland committed—even the business men and the strong farmers and the clerics—committed to the policy of Sinn Féin on a separatist basis, was never seriously entertained by anybody. [I know that there are some now who will tell you that they always expected it, but I know also that they are liars: *they did not*]. Griffith, I know, never expected it. I remember, away back about 1905 or 1906, at the time the Sinn Féin League and the Dungannon Clubs and the National Council were being amalgamated, and it was a question whether the constitution of the amalgamated organisation should be a rigidly separatist one or whether it should cover also the Dual Monarchy idea, Griffith saying, at one of the many private arguments of that time, that the mass of the people were not separatists, and would not actively support a rigidly separatist policy. Many of us did not agree with him, but we did agree that the prospect of their doing so was sufficiently remote to warrant us in agreeing to a constitution for the Sinn Féin organisation which would enable the separatist to interpret it as a separatist constitution, and the "Patriot Parliament" man to interpret it as based on the Dual Monarchy as a minimum. We who had been concerned in the fight for life of the separatist idea from 1898 on to 1916 had been too long fighting for life to give much thought to so complete a victory as the movement achieved in 1918. We did hope eventually to win enough elections to react vitally on the general bearing and progress of the nation, but we were honest enough with ourselves not to delude ourselves with dreams of victory, and to remember that what our political lives held for us in the future, as in the past, was hard work and no thanks.

The victory of Christmas, 1918, was not a victory of conviction, but of emotion. It was a victory occasioned less by any sudden achievement by the majority of a belief in Ireland a Nation than by the sudden reaction against various acts of English tyranny; and such of us as gave the movement any thought at all knew, and freely expressed it privately, that it depended altogether on England whether we maintained and consolidated the position or not. Father O'Flanagan made at the time a remark, in an after-victory speech, which deserves to be recorded, it was so wise and profound and so utterly lost in the emotional enthusiasm of the time. "The people," said he, "have voted Sinn Féin, What we have to do now is to explain to them what Sinn Féin is." It was what we did not do.

For the best part of a generation the dream of Sinn Féin had been a Government or Parliament on the model of Thomas Davis's projected "Council of Three Hundred," a sort of *de jure* Parliament to which the Irish people should give allegiance and which would direct and marshal them in the effort to assert their rights. It was, therefore, a foregone conclusion that after the 1918 victory, the newly-elected Members of Parliament would meet in Ireland and declare themselves to be the lawful governing authority of the Irish people, and attempt to form a polity within a polity. They met accordingly—such of them as were not in prison—on the 21st January, 1919, at the Mansion House, affirmed Ireland's right to and reassertion of her claim to independence, ratified the establishment of the Irish Republic, and adopted a message to the nations of the world formally notifying them of Ireland's re-entry as a nation. It was the beginning of Dáil Eireann, and the end of an epoch, the end of the epoch of Irish subservience to England, the end of the period during which the Irish people were faced by their greatest danger, the danger of complete assimilation to English civilisation. On January 21st, 1919, Ireland finally came clear of all that, and stood out on her own feet. Whatever happened to the actual movement itself, after that the old policy and the old position were impossible. The future was with the Separatists.

CHAPTER VII.

THE SINN FEIN POLICY IN PRACTICE.

Sinn Féin had won the Election of 1918 on two things—on its appeal to the Peace Conference and on its promise to set up in Ireland a Government which should actually function independently of English recognition of it; and the first tasks of Dáil Eireann were concerned with these two propositions. So far as the Peace Conference was concerned, it was all waste labour, and might just as well have been recognised as such at the beginning. We never had a chance of getting into the Peace Conference, but the whole campaign undoubtedly was a help to Ireland from the view-point of foreign propaganda. The rendering powerless of English government here was the real Sinn Féin policy, and it was vigorously pushed as the Peace Conference receded.

Even now, looking back at it in cold blood, looking over all that has happened, all the bloodshed, treachery, and sickening hypocrisy of the last two years, the abiding impression is the impression of the courage and magnificence of the gesture which threw down openly and composedly a challenge to the greatest Empire the world has seen. That is what Sinn Féin did. It declared to the British that they had no claim to Ireland which was not rendered null and void by the Irish people's definite repudiation of any such claim, and that the only just and constitutional government in Ireland was the Government of Dáil Eireann, which was elected by the people and represented the people. There is no gesture in history quite so magnificent, quite so proud as that; and nothing that has happened can take away from it. It was not a challenge to a decadent Empire, not a challenge to an Empire beset with enemies, as was Deak's challenge to Austria, but a challenge to an Empire that had just emerged triumphantly as the victor from the greatest war in history, an Empire that nowhere on earth, save in Ireland, had an enemy that dared say "boo." We had thrown down that challenge when it was still doubtful to what extent England would emerge unscathed from the Great War, but we renewed it and strengthened it when she had emerged the victor. Who does not remember the first Mansion House public meeting after the Armistice, with Sinn Féin's message to the people: "The Great War is over, but the Little War is only beginning"? And so it proved.

The Sinn Féin policy in actual practice proved itself to be the magnificent instrument which Griffith and others claimed it would be. In a year it undid much of the evil caused to the nation by a century of attendance at the British Parliament, and in two years it made British government in Ireland practically ineffective and, what was better, made it look ridiculous. Dáil Eireann had been justified and strengthened. At first the British looked on and tried to ignore what was happening, but very quickly they recognised the significance of it and tried to suppress what they could not trick. But it made no difference. The Government of Dáil was no less real because it governed "on the run," and with the increasing use of coercion came its answer—war.

Sinn Féin, in its day of triumph, did what in its day of weakness it said it would do if Ireland trusted it. It took Ireland out of the ditch and set her up among the nations. When it established Dáil Eireann it set up what had not been in Ireland for centuries, a native Parliament with the full authority of the Irish people behind it; and the very establishment of that authoritative assembly had the effect which Sinn Féin had foretold it would have. It concentrated Irish attention on the Irish Parliament; and nothing was more remarkable, in the course of the struggle, than the way in which, month after month, the number of people giving allegiance to the Irish Government, accepting it, and recognising that British Government of Ireland was over, grew. Nothing hampered that growth, neither political error nor political set-back, until, at the end, Dáil stood with the whole people behind it, passively if you like but still with it, save a very small active minority of the old garrison element.

Having set up its national assembly, Sinn Féin proceeded to make its government effective. It captured the local Councils, as well as the Parliamentary representation, and through these directed local government in the country. It established abroad Irish representatives who helped to bring Ireland back into European calculations. It established Arbitration Courts to which the people brought large numbers of cases which, in the ordinary course, would have gone to the British Courts. It butted in on education, and on everything; and under its guidance the people made British law inoperative, save where it could be enforced by armed soldiers or police. It brought the people to the point that they gave their authority and their allegiance to Dáil Eireann, obeyed it and recognised it and helped it, suffered British government but did not recognise it and did not help it. It brought about a situation wherein we had in Ireland two governments; one, our own, which was effective, but outlawed; and the other, which had all the outward machinery of government but nobody to govern, its effective authority being confined to its own armed forces—an army confessedly in hostile country—and a small proportion of the native population. It drove home to everybody in Ireland the fact that the British Government in Ireland was an alien and an unconstitutional government. In effect, it ousted it, and there was nothing left to England but "force, force to the utmost, force to the uttermost."

The Sinn Féin policy demonstrated, in actual practice, that no country can be held by another country against its determined will, unless that other country is prepared to resort to wholesale slaughter. If the people of a country will neither work, nor help, nor suffer a foreign government, that foreign government cannot function outside its own actual machine. And in that sense the victory of Sinn Féin in Ireland was a world happening. It demonstrated to all subject nations that there was a way to paralyse any foreign government, provided the people were sufficiently determined and sufficiently united to take it.

CHAPTER VIII.

THE BLACK-AND-TAN WAR.

The organisation of the Irish Volunteers had progressed with
the growth of Sinn Féin; and with the establishment by Sinn
Féin of a national Government, the Volunteers prepared to
defend that Government. They had arms and the will to use
them if necessary; and when it became clear that England
meant to suppress Dáil and all it stood for by force, the
Volunteers prepared to use that force. It is questionable
whether the Irish people, when they voted Sinn Féin, knew
they were voting for war; it is questionable whether, if they
did, they would have so voted; but the actual growth of war
was so gradual as to be almost imperceptible, and as it was
preceded by patent and challenging aggression and use of
military force by England, the actual operations of war did not
shake the hold of Sinn Féin on the people. On the contrary,
they rather strengthened it. The war was obviously and clearly
a defensive war, and a defensive war which was waged with
remarkable skill and success.

The harrying of Dáil, the attempts at arrest of such men as
Collins, Brugha and Mulcahy, and general preparations indi-
cated that military measures were about to be taken. They
were met in the first instance by an attack on the "eyes and
ears" of the British in Ireland, the Royal Irish Constabulary,
and detective and special forces. Cork began it with the shooting of a man named Quinless, an ex-member of Casement's
Brigade, who had been foolish enough to get in touch both
with the Castle and with the Volunteers, and was attempting
to betray one to the other—which to which is not certain. But

anyway the Cork Volunteers took no chances with him. That was followed in Dublin by the shooting of some of the most active and obnoxious of the members of the "G" Division— the plain-clothes division—of the Dublin Metropolitan Police. And that by the ambushing at Soloheadbeg in Tipperary of a party of police escorting munitions. That policy spread all over Ireland, and, in particular, there was a general attack upon police and police barracks. The result of it was that the police had to be withdrawn from the country districts and concentrated in the towns; and that even there the risks of being actively anti-Irish were so great that the majority of them, while carrying out orders, literally gave no effective help to the British, and the army found that it must organise its own police and its own intelligence. The result was an influx of British Secret Service men, of English and Scottish recruits for the R.I.C., to whom the name of Black-and-Tans was given, and lastly the establishment of the Auxiliaries—side by side, of course, with an enormous increase in the regular army. They were all of no avail. Each new measure was met and held.

No more heroic nor more apparently hopeless struggle was ever waged than that which the Irish Volunteers waged in 1920 and 1921. Their numbers were limited. Their equipment was more limited. They carried their lives in their hands at all times. Save at such times as they carried out operations, they had to lie hidden. But their courage was tremendous, and they waged their guerilla war against all odds and stuck it out against all odds. In the end the troops had to go about in protected cages, for they never knew when or where they might be ambushed, and their intelligence failed to afford them any protection. The many surprise hold-ups carried out in Dublin by troops and auxiliaries were always unlucky, from their point of view, and the ambushing went on, and got worse.

But Cork, the centre of the martial law area, and the headquarters of General Strickland and of the main British forces, was the centre of the war, and it did the heaviest and the most successful fighting. I remember when martial law was proclaimed, after everything had been suppressed, and when it was decreed that anybody found with arms in a martial law

area, or anybody giving help or shelter to such a person, would
be shot, how depressed everybody was. Within a few days
Cork answered the new coercion with the biggest battle that
had up to then occurred, when seven lorry-loads of Auxiliaries
were met and shot to pieces near Macroom, only one lorry
getting back to tell the story. It was followed by other fights
equally comforting, and the depression passed. In the rest of
Ireland, outside Dublin, Clare, Tipperary, Limerick, and part
of Mayo, there was very little real activity, sustained activity;
and the brunt of the war fell upon Cork, and the British effort
was concentrated upon Cork. At first General Strickland guaranteed to have Cork quiet by Christmas, 1920; then he postponed his date to the 1st April, 1921; but the 1st April came to
find him April fool, and the date was postponed indefinitely.

As the war progressed it grew savage. The British forces
became brutal. They committed many foul murders of civilians
and of Volunteers who had surrendered, much arson, much
looting, and in general established a reign of terror. But they
failed to shake the people or to break the people. *They* helped
the Volunteers, sheltered them, gave them food, and money to
buy munitions, and took their risks. And so long as they held
firm, the Volunteers could not be beaten, and were not beaten.

All this while Dáil Eireann functioned and its Government
governed. It met in secret, though every meeting was a widely-
known secret, widely-known and widely-kept. And according
as the country was cleared of police, Dáil Eireann stepped in
and established its courts and its local government, until at the
end, British government in Ireland was a mere framework of
army, police, and officials; and according as Dáil demonstrated
that it was governing, that it had the will and the grit to go on
governing, its hold on the country strengthened. In any country
people will naturally tend to rally to a native authority, and it
was remarkable in the course of evolution of Dáil, how those
classes in Ireland which were pro-British and inimical to Sinn
Féin, came at first to recognise that Dáil was governing, and
at last actually to recognise its authority. And it was that
which finally broke England's will to war, the fact that her
government in Ireland had been driven out of the country

save in so far as it had a guard of soldiers around it, and that Dáil had established its authority over the mass of the people and was not alone a *de jure* Government but throughout most of the country a *de facto* Government also.

The war which the Volunteers waged was unique in guerilla warfare. The general attack upon the police in the country districts, and the burning of their barracks cleared the open country of British forces, save those forces which remained in certain "key" towns, and such as traversed the country roads in lorries. That left the British without eyes and ears in the country. In Dublin, where all the badly-wanted Headquarters men remained to the end, and to which the badly-wanted country men freely resorted, the early elimination of the aggressive men of the G Division had resulted in the Dublin Metropolitan Police confining itself to police duties, and keeping clear of anything which would commit it to the political issue. So that in Dublin also the British were without eyes and ears, and were dependent on imported Secret Service men. The Black-and-Tans, Auxiliaries, and regular soldiers there were met and were held by the Ambush policy, a thing which, carried out on the scale on which it was carried out, was totally new in warfare. Mobile bodies of Volunteers, small in number, inadequately armed with revolvers, home-made bombs, and a very occasional machine-gun, resisted all the efforts of the British to round them up, or to impair their organisation. With the support of the mass of the people they were enabled to defy every effort made to break them up. It was not a case of a small mobile force keeping to the hills and maintaining itself in inaccessible places, but a case of the Volunteers honeycombing the places which were most strongly held by the British, in addition to maintaining bodies on the hills. And it was the support of the civil population which made this possible. The men on the run could not have escaped arrest for a week were it not for the fact that the civil population was solidly behind them, and not alone refused to help the British, but passively obstructed them.

CHAPTER IX..

THE NEW GRIFFITH.

In the evolution of Dáil Eireann Mr. de Valera counted for very little. He was in prison when it was established, and shortly after his escape from prison he went to America, where he remained until the war was almost over. Griffith counted more, but he also was in prison when Dáil was established, and he was in prison again when the truce came. The movement as a whole—Dáil and the Irish Volunteers—was run by the men who kept out of prison all the time, that is, by Mick Collins, Cathal Brugha, and the Headquarters Staff of the Irish Volunteers. In actual practice, Mick Collins was, in effect, a dictator.

The Griffith of these years was not the old Griffith, not the pre-1916 Griffith. In the early struggling years of Sinn Féin, he had been confident of his own power, happy in his own leadership, and he had distrusted every attempt by any Sinn Féin group to strike out any independent line of action. He had seen his way, then, to a resurrection of Ireland on the Sinn Féin policy outlined by him, a policy which was essentially constructive, educative, and based upon moral force and passive resistance, rather than on physical force. He had believed, then, that Ireland, organised as he could organise her on the Sinn Féin policy basis, could force England to grant her everything except complete separation; and it was because the Dual Monarchy solution provided the only solution which would satisfy Ireland's national honour and, at the same time, save England's face, that he fought so resolutely to have it made the basis of the early Sinn Féin organisation. He never faltered in that belief, though his robust optimism in the future of Sinn Féin was rather shaken by the failure of the Sinn Féin daily and the decay of the organisation in the years after 1909. Then came the Irish Volunteers and the Rising. Griffith was, of course, heart and soul with the Volunteers, but, in common with ninety-nine per cent. of the population of Ireland, he was against the Rising. It cut across his conception of an orderly and evolutionary movement, and the consequences of a bad failure were always present in his mind. He was not out in Easter Week, and after the great change came, when the people who would have torn the "Seven" to pieces during Easter Week if they could have got hold of them, began to shout about what *they* had done in the Rising, Griffith was violently attacked, and defended, for not having been out. The attackers said he had funked the fight, and the defenders said that he had been ordered to stand aside by the Seven. He never alluded to it himself, as far as I know, and the truth probably is that he regarded the Rising as a blunder and kept out of it. But in any case, he never afterwards displayed the same determination in keeping his place and his authority in the movement, and though he must have been convinced that the physical force side of the movement was jeopardising everything, he made no attempt to control it, and let the physical force men have full sway. The success of the Rising, and its aftermath in bringing the people of Ireland over to a separatist policy, a success which he knew could not have been obtained in two generations by ordinary propaganda, silenced him in so far as questions of policy involving physical force were concerned; and he no more dared than anybody else to point out that a second Rising would largely undo the first. He went with the tide, and it speedily became a red tide.

Griffith was not fond of me. He never knew when I might do or say something which would place the movement in a different light from that in which he viewed it. But we were always friendly, and on one occasion when I wrote to him from England during my deportation, he surprised me by writing me a letter very appreciative of my services to the cause. In the years of the war I saw very little of him, but one of the few conversations I did have with him threw, to me, a lot of light on his outlook at the time. In May, 1920, I had to go to Cork, and was asked by Terry MacSwiney to leave a few days after I had arrived. He would not at first tell me why; but as I refused to budge, he told me of a certain proposal which was probably being put into operation in a few days, and for which I would probably be picked up if I were in the city when it happened. The proposal seemed to me then to be fiendish and indefensible and inadvisable from any point of view, and it still seems so to me. He said to me that they were only awaiting sanction from Headquarters, and I felt easier, saying to him that they would never sanction that. However, in a couple of days the messenger arrived back with sanction. I returned to Dublin at once and went to Griffith. I told him what the proposal was, that it had been sanctioned, gave him my opinion of it, and added that I assumed he knew nothing of it. He said to me that he had not been consulted, that the Dáil Cabinet had not, as far as he knew, been consulted, that he agreed with me about it, and that he would see Brugha and stop it, which he did. I said to him then: "I don't know what are the relations between the Dáil Cabinet and the Volunteers, but you are Acting-President of Dáil and the country will hold you responsible for what happens. You ought to see that nothing of this sort is sanctioned by anybody without the Dáil Cabinet being first consulted. If you don't control the Volunteers, they will bring us all down in red ruin." To that he made no direct answer, and I did not expect one; but after a minute or so he said, in that cold reflective way of his "The military mind is the same in every country. Our military men are as bad as the British. They think of nothing but their own particular end, and cannot be brought to consider the political consequences of their pro-proceedings."

There is not much in that, on the surface, but to one who had known Griffith, and worked with him and been intimate with his mind and thought as I had been, it contained everything. It told me that Griffith was profoundly uneasy at the red orientation which the movement was making, and at the same time that either he was not strong enough in his influence in Dáil, or not determined enough in himself, to make an effort to regulate and control the Volunteers while still there was time.

I believe that the shooting and the ambushing and the savagery and moral collapse which they generated, sickened his soul and then his body; I believe that he was glad that the responsibility for the leadership was not on his shoulders, and that the red policy had been begun while he was in prison; I believe that he stuck to his post and his limited leadership solely out of a sense of duty and of service, and that when that last chance came of an honourable way out, he threw the last ounce of his strength into the effort to secure it for his country.

CHAPTER X.

THE CRIME OF THE ULSTER BOYCOTT.

One of the fundamental principles of intellectual nationalism in the nineteenth century had been the unity and oneness of Ireland. The Northern Irishmen, whose forefathers had been United Irishmen almost to a man, were looked upon as being erring Irishmen, but as Irishmen. Sinn Féin had accepted that principle also, and all its early work and plans were based upon the oneness of Ireland. But now, when Sinn Féin represented the Irish majority, and swayed it more absolutely than it had been swayed since O'Connell had swayed it, it amazed those who had been working in it since the beginning by throwing overboard the fundamental principle of the union of all Irishmen, and declaring that the Ulster Irishman was a foreigner. It was no longer, clearly, a movement, but a political party.

The policy of dividing Irishmen was always one of England's main reliances in holding Ireland, and right up to the end she pursued it. In all the preoccupation of the war, her statesmen and her makers of public opinion never forgot that in 1914 the Irish Parliamentary Party had accepted the principle of partition, and that in 1916 a Convention of the nationalists of Ulster had accepted it. "Whatever happens in the future," said the *Times,* "that stands." And England kept it always in her mind. She was helped by both sides in Ireland, and by circumstances arising out of the war. The war, by demonstrating that the Ulster majority and the Irish majority were on opposite sides in a matter which both regarded as vital, made what had not been here up to then, a real breach between the two sides, a consciousness of difference. The Ulster majority had, and has, no more love for England or the English than the Irish majority; and the Ulster majority is as Irish, as distinct and separate from the English, as is the Irish majority, but it had taken a side in which it believed, and it fought on that side; and when the casualty lists came and it suffered, it began to think itself different from the Irish majority. Figures have, I know, been quoted to show that the other three provinces contributed as large a proportion of their population to the British armies as did Ulster. But these figures are beside the point. In the one case the contribution was made publicly and with general acclamation and approval; and in the other it was made secretly almost, and in the face of general apathy where there was not active disapproval. That it was, the spirit, the viewpoint, which made the difference, and not the respective contributions of man-power. On top of that came the Rising, which the Ulster majority regarded as unjustifiable treachery, and on top of that came the boycott.

The Ulster movement on which Sir Edward Carson rose to fame, and which ended in the establishment of a separate Government for six Ulster counties, was never intended to lead to that. The Ulster majority did not want partition; up to the very end they disliked it, and they adopted it only very grudgingly; but circumstances, English policy, and the swash-buckling stupidity of the new leaders of the Irish majority, forced them to partition as the only thing which would give them that security which they did not think they could rely upon from an All-Ireland Government.

The history of the boycott is instructive. Feeling in the South had been getting up against Belfast since the Belfast and Derry riots of 1919, and it was inflamed by certain Northern Nationalists who had been forced, by the destruction of their businesses and by imminent danger to their lives to fly from Belfast to Dublin, and who forgot everything there except their thirst for revenge upon Belfast. The boycott itself started in the town of Tuam, where the local traders and others banded together and decided to boycott all Belfast commercial travellers and goods until the expelled Nationalists should be reinstated. From Tuam the idea spread to Dublin, where the aforesaid refugee Nationalists pushed it vigorously, and where a certain amount of unofficial boycotting began to show itself. The idea of an official boycott was raised in Dáil, and although—astonishing fact—it was supported by Griffith, the opinion of Dáil was against it, and a division was avoided by an agreement to leave the question over for consideration and decision by the Dáil Cabinet. And in the Cabinet, Griffith's influence finally prevailed, and the boycott was officially decreed, promulgated, and enforced. It was at first nominally restricted to Belfast and to a few firms outside Belfast; but it was gradually extended, and in practice it was applied to the whole of Unionist Ulster.

The boycott itself was not the worst of the new situation. It was the things which it produced that did the damage. It raised up in the South what never had been there, a hatred of the North, and a feeling that the North was as much an enemy of Ireland as was England. It made Protestant Home Rulers in the North almost ashamed of their principles, and it turned apathetic Protestant Unionists into bitter partisans. It gave the irresponsibles in the South their first taste of loot and destruction, when it used the Irish Volunteers in destroying Belfast cigarettes in small shops in Dublin, and in intercepting and destroying Belfast goods on the railways. It recognised and established real partition, spiritual and voluntary partition, before physical partition had been established and while it was still very doubtful whether it ever would be established. It denied the whole principle upon which separatists of every generation had claimed for the people of this country—independence. And it was absolutely ineffective. It inflicted more harm upon the Nationalists of Ulster, who had to suffer while theorists here howled hatred and boycott from a safe distance outside; it probably inflicted some damage on the Ulster majority, but it was an utter failure inasmuch as it did not secure the reinstatement of a single expelled Nationalist, nor the conversion of a single Unionist. It was merely a blind and suicidal contribution to the general hate.

There is not a word to be said in favour of the Ulster Boycott. It is an utterly shameful episode in the history of Sinn Féin.

CHAPTER XI.

THE MORAL COLLAPSE.

Sinn Féin, in its pre-1916 days, was a simple, straight-forward, and essentially moral movement. It was a movement composed, in the main, of people with high ideals, who worked very hard in it and neither received nor expected anything in return. It was ascetic and clean, and its personnel corresponded to its ideals. Its material was good, and its influence was all good.

When it swept the country, it swept into itself a great deal of bad material, drunkards and crooks and morally unsuitable people of all sorts. These people percolated it, and affected it even though they did not control it. They had a bad effect upon it, and through it upon the people as a whole; and, that lowering of its moral was contributed to also by the failure of the civil side of the movement to exercise control over the military side, and by the assumption by the Irish Volunteers of the power of life and death in the country, without reference to the civil side of the movement, which had to bear the responsibility for the political consequences of many acts not authorised by it nor liked by it.

There came to every combatant nation during the War, a moral coarseness, hardness, callousness, which Ireland escaped. When the Great War ended in November, 1918, human life was as sacred in Ireland as it had been in 1914; but that state of things did not long survive the operations of the gunman in the Little War. The first shootings stirred and shocked the public conscience tremendously; but as they became more common, as the British failed completely to bring anybody to

book for them, and as the shooting evolved until it became a
guerilla war, the public conscience grew to accept it as the
natural order of things. The public conscience as a whole was
never easy about it, and would have been glad at any time to
stop it, but it never got any farther than that. It was not organised, and the things that were organised gave it no clear lead,
for the national Press sat on the fence, and such Churchmen
as condemned the shootings mixed their ethics with politics and
made the case worse. The eventual result of that was a complete moral collapse here. When it was open to any Volunteer
Commandant to order the shooting of any civilian, and to
cover himself with the laconic legend "Spy" on the dead man's
breast, personal security vanished and no man's life was safe.
And when it was possible for the same Commandant to steal
goods and legalise it by calling it "commandeering," and to
burn and destroy goods and legalise that by saying they were
Belfast or English goods, social security vanished. With the
vanishing of reason and principle and morality we became
a mob, and a mob we remained. And for the mob there is
only one law—gun law. So the gunman became supreme;
and the only thing which counted in Ireland, in anything,
was force; for the spirit of the gunman invaded everything,
not politics alone. Thenceforward there was no consideration
and no reason and no argument—nothing but blind obedience
to somebody above, whether Dáil Cabinet or Volunteers'
Executive. When the Belfast boycott was introduced, for
instance, attempts to discuss it were met with horror at a Sinn
Féin branch, and with the information that this was "an order
from Dáil Eireann" and therefore not for discussion or
question.

As the war lengthened, it became more brutal and more
savage and more hysterical and more unrelievedly black. But
its worst effect was on the women. They were the first to be
thrown off their base, and, as the war lengthened, they steadily
deteriorated. They took to their hearts every catch-cry and
every narrowness and every bitterness, and steadily eliminated
from themselves every womanly feeling. Women in politics
was no new thing in Ireland. In Sinn Féin itself they had

always worked side by side with the men, and in the early Sinn Féin days there had been a woman's organisation—Inginidhe na hEireann—founded by Maud Gonne, which had been active and useful. But its work had been social and constructive, and it had never forgot that there was special work which men could not do but which it could, just as it never forgot that it could not and should not do men's work. It did such useful, commonplace, and unrhetorical work as looking after poor children, and things like that, as well as its share of the constructive political propaganda and political work which was then being done. But Cumann na mBhan, the women's organisation of the later Sinn Féin knew better than that. It organised itself on a "military" basis, got itself uniforms, called itself "Commandant" and "Captain," threw overboard construction and devoted itself to destruction. Woman's business in the world is with the things of life, with the things that make life; but these women busied themselves with nothing but the things of death—first-aid, bandages, splints, gunshot wounds and broken limbs and broken bodies—these were their occupation and their delight. They learned, too, how to clean a weapon, in many cases how to handle it, and in the last stages, each branch (miscalled a "Company") was solemnly attached to a Volunteer Company and was supposed to attend it when going into action. Thus, in the worst phases of the war, Dublin was full of hysterical women, living on excitement, enjoying themselves in the thought of ambushes and *stunts*, stifling their consciences with the parrot cry, "Nothing matters but to support the army"—when the thing which really mattered was to *control* the army—cutting themselves loose from everything which their sex contributes to civilisation and social order. Just as, on the male side, the gunman came to be the dominant personality, so also his counterpart, the gunwoman, came to be the dominating figure of the women's side of the movement. The gunwoman lived on war, on excitement, on stunts, and gradually shut out everything but those. She saw nobody, talked to nobody, save other gunwomen, lived for nothing save war, and came at the last to be incapable of realising an Ireland without it. War, and the things which war breeds—intolerance, swagger, hardness, unwomanliness—captured the women, turned them into unlovely, destructive-minded, arid begetters of violence, both physical violence and mental violence.

CHAPTER XII.

THE SURRENDER OF ENGLAND.

To an Ireland in the grip of England there were always two policies open, the policy of constructive passive resistance—the Sinn Féin policy—and the Fenian policy of physical force. The first of these proved itself to be a defence upon which England could make no impression. As fast as she took away leaders, others stepped into their places, and the work of establishing a *de jure* government and of making that government function went on unchecked, until over the majority of the country it was a *de facto* government as well, and the British Government was only a name and an army, for the teeth of its police force, which was always its standby, had been drawn. Its attempts to suppress Dáil Eireann by process of law, by show of constitutional authority, failed, and its every proceeding against Sinn Féin had boomeranged against itself. The influence and power of Sinn Féin steadily increased, and were solidified by the fact that against its programme and its Government, England had nothing to put up except the Partition Act of 1920, which nobody in Ireland wanted and which everybody in Ireland detested. Beyond that she had nothing to offer Ireland except constitutional coercion, backed up by the threat of physical coercion at the first available opportunity. Failing that opportunity, Ireland was lost to her; but, given that opportunity, there was still a chance that she might recover her hold and maintain it.

When, therefore, the attempt to undermine Sinn Féin constitutionally failed, England adopted a policy of provoking the Irish Volunteers to another insurrection, in the hope that in the

red ruin and slaughter which would follow a regular insurrection, she would crush out the brain as well as the muscle
of the movement, and teach Ireland a final lesson. It was the
Tory Irish policy—the policy recommended to England in
1916 by the *Irish Times*—which, however, it only nibbled at
without fully adopting. The goad was therefore applied: Dáil
Eireann suppressed, the Sinn Féin organisation suppressed,
the Irish Volunteers suppressed, Cumann na mBhan suppressed,
and eventually even the Gaelic League and the Gaelic Athletic
Association. To the suppressed but very much alive movement, all Nationalist Ireland and much of Unionist Ireland
rallied. Then the Royal Irish Constabulary were encouraged
to assassinate Sinn Féin leaders, and they made a beginning
in Cork by the assassination of Tomás Mac Curtin, then Lord
Mayor of Cork, and followed it up in other cases. We, on
our side, helped to swell the blood river by the elimination of
the Dublin G-men, the shooting of spies, and the general
suppression of civil authority by the gun. Ambush and battle,
and reprisal and counter-reprisal followed, but the British
were held. They had planned to provoke an insurrection, and
instead they got a war, a war which in its evolution owed
something to chance but more to design, which constantly
harassed the enemy but never gave him formal battle. And
by this time Mick Collins dominated the whole movement.
The Irish Republican Brotherhood and the Irish Volunteers'
Executives had become mere machines for registering his
plans, and through the group more particularly attached to
him he controlled also Dáil Eireann and Sinn Féin. Every
thread was in the one strong unselfish hand—deservedly so, for
Mick had proved himself to be the one man who could co-
ordinate and wield the whole machine.

As the war lengthened it grew more savage and more
destructive, and the general public liked it less and less. With
a growing admiration for and support for the Volunteers,
there went a growing uneasiness as to the final outcome, a
growing irritation at some of the military operations. In Dublin,
for instance, the public resentment against the callousness of
continual ambushes in "the Dardanelles" and in other crowded

streets, with heavy casualties to civilians, was deep and deepening, but it was accompanied by no weakening of the general support accorded to the main position.

In the summer of 1921, the prospect was of the blackest. On the military side there was a shortage of arms and of ammunition, a very grievous shortage, and in addition, there was increased British activity and a general circumscribing of the area within which the various Volunteer units could operate. In Cork, which was the main battle area, operating was getting very difficult, and the position in the country as a whole was worsening. On the civil side, the strain was telling. The strain on the military man was slight. Save during an operation he lay hidden in some secure place, or comparatively free in territory where there were no British; but the civilian worker—the Dáil Minister or official, the Irish Volunteers' Headquarters Executive, for instance—cooped up in Dublin, felt the strain. And the ordinary civilian, the man who minded his job, was searched regularly in the streets, never knew when he might run into a Volunteer's bomb or an "Auxy's" revolver; who had to stand behind his desk or counter although five minutes before there had been an ambush outside his window, and although he knew that in five minutes more he might be "plugged" by the irate Auxiliaries or he might be being tortured in Dublin Castle by the Intelligence Officers there, disliked the prospect more and more. He had supported Sinn Féin on general principles, because he believed in an Irish Republic, but he had supported the Republican programme without in any way believing that Ireland could get independence this time, but in the belief and hope that the pushing of the full demand would lead to something very substantial. And at this juncture all he could see was that both sides were shooting and illtreating each other like savages, that the ordinary citizen received little consideration from either, that public confidence and trade were being very adversely affected by the long continuance of the war, and that unless it was stopped there would be a general collapse. And of a stoppage there was no sign.

And then, then when the outlook was at its blackest, England surrendered. King George's speech at Belfast on the

22nd June, 1921, and Mr. Lloyd George's letter to Mr. de Valera of the 24th June, 1921, surrendered Ireland. They said, in effect, "All right, we give in. We've had enough. But we must save our face. We cannot recognise a Republic, but we can do almost anything short of that."

That was the plain political meaning of it. The greatest Empire of modern times, at the height of its power and strength, went down on its knees to a little nation and begged for terms. There is no parallel to that in ancient or modern history. Ireland had won her fight.

To grasp the full magnitude of it, one has only to compare the terms of the Irish Truce with the terms of the Armistice which Germany accepted at the close of the Great War. She had to surrender her arms, surrender territory, and submit to many humiliations. She was treated as a vanquished enemy. Whereas we, on the other hand, were treated as England's equal, and agreed to no conditions for our Volunteers which England did not also agree to for her army. In Tom Kettle's phrase:

> "Soldier with equal soldier *did* we sit
> Closing a battle, not forgetting it
> With not one name to hide."

And when our plenipotentiaries sat down across a table to discuss terms, they sat on equal terms and talked on equal terms, and signed eventually as one sovereign nation with another sovereign nation.

It was a tremendous and a heartening moral victory, a victory which, rightly used, would have placed Ireland first among European nations in the things that really mattered. It came when the nation was strung up to a high pitch of emotional intensity, and it put the people into a plastic mood in which they might have been moulded in any way our leaders pleased. Every omen was favourable. The events of the "Tan" war had alienated from England the sympathy of the mass of the old Unionist elements. When the Truce came, these at once realised what it meant—the victory of the Irish language, culture and traditions. They at once knew the sort of new Ireland they might expect. And they started to prepare for that new Ireland by learning Irish. The last six months of 1921 saw a phenomenal increase in the sale of Irish grammars, dictionaries, and primers of all sorts. We had a united people and an enthusiastic people, and a people flowing over with good-will; and the reactions of the moral weakening I have referred to in the previous chapter need never have had other than individual consequences. But when Mr. de Valera made the split he demolished all that. Away went the Irish primers, and the unity, and the enthusiasm, and the good-will. And away went the possibility of confining the moral havoc within minimum limits. The moral corner-stone was out. and our edifice fell to pieces.

But for all that the main achievement stands to our credit, to be seen in its full impressiveness only by future generations. We had done what Germany failed to do—brought England to her knees.

CHAPTER XIII.

THE TRUCE.

The period following on Mr. Lloyd George's letter to Mr. de Valera was a period of tense silence in Ireland. The people waited, strung up to a fever pitch, hardly daring to draw their breath, waiting to see what Mr. de Valera's answer would be. When that answer was not a definite refusal—as it would have been had either Mr. de Valera or his Cabinet meant to hold out for independence—a sigh of relief went up from the majority of the people. They knew, then, that it was peace, that the war was over, and that normal life was coming again. And the crowd of people assembled around the Mansion House, who cheered General Macready when he went into the Mansion House to confer with representatives of Dáil, were cheering, not him nor those whom he represented, but the great fact that here was the end of the Terror, and not alone of the Terror but of everything evil which the political struggle against England had brought with it. The Volunteers became popular heroes, and their leaders began to get swelled heads.

The suggestion, afterwards made, that Messrs. de Valera, Brugha, and Stack did not realise that they were committing themselves to a compromise when they stopped the war and toyed with the British proposal, is one which is insulting to any man with intelligence and honesty. The details of the Cabinet discussion on it are not known, but when Mr. de Valera made a pronouncement, that pronouncement was perfectly clear. He invited the Ulster Unionists and the Southern Unionists respectively to send someone to confer with him so that a common policy for Ireland might be framed and presented to

Mr. Lloyd George. Is anybody so foolish as to believe, or to expect others to believe, that when Mr. de Valera issued that invitation, he contemplated Sir James Craig and Lord Midleton subscribing their names to a demand for complete independence? Is anybody so foolish as to believe that Mr. de Valera ever meant to ask them to do so? Sir James Craig refused to confer, but Lord Midleton and other Southern Unionists did confer with Mr. de Valera, and, as far as we know, satisfactorily. Is anybody so foolish as to believe that Mr. de Valera induced Lord Midleton to agree to a demand for complete independence, or that he even asked him to agree to such a demand? Mr. de Valera then went to see Mr. Lloyd George, and was closeted with him daily for a week. Is anybody so foolish as to believe that they were discussing independence? Is anybody so foolish as not to believe that Mr. de Valera, at the interviews, ascertained exactly how far England was prepared to go, and that, when he later ordered Griffith and Collins to go over and negotiate a treaty, he knew exactly the sort of treaty they would get?

The truth is, that once the war was stopped and the Truce agreed to and negotiations begun, there was no alternative to the acceptance of the best terms that could be screwed out of England. The Volunteers were, of course, quite willing to fight again; but they would not have had the support of the people in a fight after refusing a reasonable offer of settlement, least of all the support of the people who, from being pro-British in 1921, were to become violent Irregulars in 1922. And the longer the Truce and the negotiations dragged on, the more impossible a renewal of the war became.

There is ample evidence that, from the beginning of the Truce, the responsible leaders, military and civil, all knew that there would be no more fighting. Men for whose photographs Dublin Castle, a few weeks before, would have given thousands, showed themselves at meetings and Aeridheachtanna, and were "snapped" by massed photographers. It was known generally and early in the negotiations that Griffith and Collins meant to make a settlement. It was known equally generally that the Headquarters Staff of the Irish Volunteers had met and had unanimously agreed "that the army would not stand in the way of a settlement." All Mr. de Valera's letters to Mr. Lloyd George were taken as twisting of the lion's tail. But, while the leaders knew that a settlement which was *not* independence was coming, they had neither the courage nor the wisdom to say so, even privately. On the contrary, they felt bound to go about pretending that the war would be renewed; encouraging bellicosity and the better organisation of bellicosity, in the belief that when they chose they could stop it; in the belief that the more bellicosity they could manufacture, the better the terms they would get.

There happened, with regard to the "Tan" war, but on a smaller scale, what had already happened with regard to Easter Week. All the counties and cities which, during the war, had taken off their hats to the District Inspector and the Colonel, and had never fired a shot, were now bursting to fight; and all the young men in all the counties who had kept aloof from the fighting when it was dangerous, were now eager to become heroes, and to be able to tell stories about this and that ambush. Instead of discouraging recruiting for the Volunteers, the leaders encouraged it; with the result that in the counties where it had been active the Volunteers' organisation was immensely strengthened, and the other counties were organised for the first time. And for the first time also they were extended into the predominatingly Unionist Ulster counties. Arms and ammunition were also bought and distributed. While Cumann na mBhan concentrated itself on making twenty thousand first-aid outfits—contemplating with enthusiasm twenty thousand approaching casualties—and on learning to shoot.

So that the Treaty was launched into an Ireland full of bellicosity, which had been unnecessarily fostered.

CHAPTER XIV.

THE GREAT BETRAYAL.

When the Treaty, signed on December 6th, 1921, was published, it was received in Ireland with mixed feelings, but the predominating opinion was that it was a far better treaty than anybody had expected, save in one particular, namely, Partition. The oath and the Governor-General, and the reservation of the possibility of an appeal to the Privy Council of England were also objectionable, but to a lesser degree; the one great blot which everybody saw being Partition. And for Partition we had largely ourselves to blame.

In the years of the fight the Sinn Féin organisation and Dáil Eireann had become a machine, in which all power and initiative were in the hands of a group, and in which independent thought and independent action were discouraged. The men who led the movement and who were responsible for the ambush policy, never expected to survive the war, never expected to win out. They put up the Republic on their banner, just as previous generations had put up independence, but they did not expect to get it. What they did expect was that their fight and their work would bring something which other men, not committed to a Republic, could use, and behind which the separatists could reform and wait. They had made no provision for victory, for sitting down with the British across a table and discussing a Treaty.

Ireland had two chances of achieving complete independence. The first was a German victory, and it was our best chance. When that failed there was one other chance, the chance that Woodrow Wilson would prove not to be the hypocrite he appeared to be and would apply his fourteen points to his allies as well as to his enemies. When that failed, there was no chance of complete independence save by forcing the British to evacuate Ireland. And it was common ground that that could only be done in the physical plane by Ireland producing a physical force greater than anything England could produce, which was obviously impossible.

Nobody realised this better than Mr. de Valera. When he came out of Lincoln Jail, for instance, he wanted to go straight to America, and not to come to Ireland at all, because he knew that if independence, with the Great War over, was to be achieved, it could only be achieved through America. In the Dáil discussions which preceded the final negotiations, he refused to be rigidly bound by his oath to the Republic, which he insisted on interpreting as an oath to do his best for the people as a whole in any emergency, and he threatened to resign if Dáil attempted to bind him to take that oath seriously. At one of the Dáil Cabinet discussions, he remarked that they were in the position of a man selling a cow, and that their job was to get a good price for the cow. A couple of days before the Treaty was signed, he was consulting various Bishops as to whether he would be justified in holding out for full fiscal powers.

When Griffith and Collins, then, signed on the 6th December, 1921, a Treaty which gave Ireland full powers, fiscal and otherwise, with a nominal oath and a nominal Governor-General to save England's face, the one person from whom they might have expected support was Mr. de Valera. He had sent them over to sign that Treaty, knowing well what it would be at its maximum, and not hoping that they would achieve the almost impossible and get that possible maximum! When they got it he stabbed them in the back by a pompous announcement that he had "recalled" the delegates, although they were already half way home. For all the bloodshed and suffering which followed, he must be held responsible. That there would be growls and objections against any Treaty which did not give Ireland complete independence was certain; but it was also certain that it was the moral support and the prestige which he gave to it which created the Anti-Treaty movement, and which were responsible for a large number of the people who went Anti-Treaty. The people wanted that Treaty, wanted it with all their hearts; and, were it not for Mr. de Valera's encouragement to the wreckers, the opposition to it would have been nominal and constitutional. I was meeting all sorts of people daily, and I know what the feeling was. Nobody loved the Treaty; everybody objected to Partition; but everybody felt that the Treaty was a tremendous achievement, and wanted it accepted and worked.

As an instance of the effect his pronouncement had, I may say this. On the morning of the publication of the news of the signature of the Treaty, I met Mary Comerford, one of the most prominent of Cumann na mBhan workers. "Have you seen the paper?" said she. "Yes." "Do you believe it?" "Of course I believe it; I told you weeks ago that something of this sort was coming." She stopped for a moment, shrugged her shoulders, and then turned away. "Ah well, all for the best. No more war." In the afternoon, Mr. de Valera's pronouncement came out, and Miss Comerford promptly embraced it. Left to herself, she would have given the Treaty a trial. So would nearly all those who, as things turned out, rallied to Mr. de Valera's hypocritical cry that he "had been betrayed."

On the contrary, he it was who was the betrayer. He knew, when he parleyed with Lloyd George, that he was breaking the Irish people's will to war, and making it impossible for the Volunteers to renew the war·with popular support. He knew right through the negotiations, from the Truce to the end, that in the end somebody would have to accept, on behalf of Ireland, the best terms which England would rise to. He knew when he asked Dáil to send plenipotentiaries who were authorised "to negotiate and sign," and when he resisted the attempt to bind them to the Republic, that he was asking Dáil to send them over to accept those best terms of England's. He knew, before he picked them, exactly how far Lloyd George would go. He knew that Collins and Griffith knew that they went over to save his face; and when they had shouldered the responsibility which their unexpected victory had thrust on Sinn Féin, when they returned with the Treaty he had sent them over to sign, he bared his teeth and rent them.

CHAPTER XV.

THE GREAT MISTAKE.

The great mistake which Sinn Féin had made was its refusal to look ahead, above all its refusal to face obvious facts and provide for them. When it went to the polls in 1918 for that General Election at which it won its first majority, it selected its candidates purely with an eye to votes. The man who was in prison, or who had been in prison, obviously had the best chance, and neither his ability nor his suitability were considered. Ability, on the contrary, was rather a disqualification, because it tended to make its possessor difficult to handle by a machine, and Sinn Féin then was rapidly becoming a machine. I had an illuminating insight into democracy in practice one day in 6 Harcourt Street. Harry Boland, who was then Secretary to Sinn Féin, was sitting at a desk as I entered, and going over a list of names. He would read out a name "John Brown. We can't have him." Then "John Black. I wonder is he safe. I'll ask X." Then "John Green. He's all right." Then he came to another list and he looked at it, and said to me: "Gavan Duffy. Do you think, P. S., that Gavan Duffy is a good Republican? Do you think we ought to let him go up?" "Well, Harry," said I, "I don't know whether he is a good Republican, and I don't know whether I am what you would call a good Republican. I prefer to call myself a separatist. But I know that Gavan Duffy was working in the separatist movement twelve years ago when it was neither popular nor respectable." "All right," said he, "I'll pass him." What he was doing, apparently, was going over the lists of proposals sent up from the constituencies, and himself deciding who would be allowed to be nominated and who would not. For the first Sinn Féin election there was a case for that. It was uncertain how many seats Sinn Féin would win, and it was vital that all the Deputies elected should be dependable and safe from the point or view of giving least trouble to the political machine. But for the second Sinn Féin election it was a different proposition. It was known then that there would not be any opposition to speak of, and it must have been plain to the leaders that at some time in its career the second Dáil would be called upon to make an arrangement with England. It was plain to me, at any rate, and it must have been equally plain to all those who had been in the old Sinn Féin movement, or who had any acquaintance with the philosophy behind the Sinn Féin policy. We had always known, and the event vindicated us, that Ireland's acquiescence in England's claim by her attendance at the English Parliament was England's real hold over Ireland, and that once the Irish people adopted the Sinn Féin policy and set up a *de jure* Irish Parliament, England would be forced to make terms. And that policy, the policy of constructive passive resistance, has since been vindicated in other countries, in Egypt for instance, and is being vindicated in India.

The case, therefore, for making the second Dáil a really representative Dáil, for including men of ability and of independent mind, was overwhelming. But it was ignored. The second Dáil was like the first—a collection of mediocrities in the grip of a machine, and leaving all its thinking to De Valera, Griffith, and Collins. It was never encouraged to think, it was never told anything but platitudes, it was given rhetoric and told how to vote. Dr. McCartan and Mr. Gavan Duffy, for instance, returning from abroad for the Dáil session which discussed the Lloyd George invitation, thought they were coming to an assembly in which thought was as free and discussion as welcome as they used to be in one of the old Sinn Féin branches. But they were amazed to find that the thing was an automatic voting machine, and that the whole Cabinet got up on its legs and barked if there was the slightest criticism of any one of them. And the same principles were applied to the appointment or Ministers. Mr. Ginnell was appointed Minister of Propaganda because he was a nuisance as an ordinary member, and Count Plunkett was appointed Minister of Fine Arts because he had to be got out of Foreign Affairs. Why he ever was appointed to Foreign Affairs, God only knows. The same principles have since been followed, with the result that the average level of ability and intelligence in the present Dáil is appallingly low, much lower than it was in the Irish Parliamentary Party.

The Dáil, then, to which the Treaty went, was a Dáil peculiarly unfitted to consider the Treaty. Its members were mere voters, and they were not representative. They did not represent the Irish people—as Mr. de Valera himself very acutely reminded them—but only one section of the people. And after having been carefully picked for their pliability, after having been fed with phrases, after having been kept absolutely in the dark as to the real position and the real opinions and plans of their leaders, the responsibility of deciding was suddenly thrust upon them, and they were hailed as men and brothers.

There were plans made to meet every situation save one, and that the one which came about and which it was obvious must come about—a request by England to sit down across a table and discuss Ireland, with complete independence barred. It is idle to think that the leaders did not know that that was coming. They did know. Informal negotiations were first opened up with Mr. Lloyd George in the autumn of 1920, and the connexion was never broken, not even by Bloody Sunday. When the thing happened which it had been known would happen, and for which no plan had been made, our leaders fumbled and were lost. They knew that complete independence was not possible, but they had not the moral courage to say so.

The path for Ireland in that situation had always been clear. History and common sense alike dictated it. Everybody who knew anything about Sinn Féin was familiar with it. The answer to Mr. Lloyd George should have been the Dual Monarchy as an irreducible minimum, and nothing else. He should have been given his choice of a Republic or a Monarchy, and the case could have been so stated that he would have found it absolutely impossible to continue war after being offered a Dual Monarchy. It was the only solution which Ireland could honourably accept, as Griffith saw years before, and it was the only solution which would make the six-county position absolutely untenable. It was the only answer to Partition. Why it was not done, I do not know; but even after the interminable letters started, the opportunity came and was lost. In Mr. Lloyd George's letter of August 13th, 1921, to Mr. de Valera, he said: "We must direct your attention to one point upon which you lay some emphasis and upon which no British Government can compromise—namely, the claim that we should acknowledge the right of Ireland to secede from her allegiance to the King. No such right can ever be acknowledged by us." The answer to that, the answer which would have at once cut away all Mr. Lloyd George's subtleties and the Six-County Parliament, was clear. It has been written across Irish Nationalist thought for two centuries, since Swift wrote it in the *Drapier's Letters*. The answer to it was: "Very well; if England insists on obliging herself to have the same King with us, Ireland will oblige herself to have the same King with England. But there is to be no subordination of Ireland. We are willing, for the sake of honourable peace, to establish a monarchy instead of a Republic, and we are willing for the sake of honourable peace to agree to have the same King with England." Lloyd George could not have gone to war against that, nor could the Six Counties have held out against it, nor could England have encouraged or helped them to hold out. Why that answer was not made, I do not know. Why the Dual Monarchy was not firmly in their minds from the first, a clear and natural solution, and an honourable solution, instead of the nebulosities of "external association," and the British Commonwealth, and a tribute to the King, and so on, I do not know. Mr. de Valera, I suppose, preferred rather to attempt to change the British Constitution than to take up that Irish Constitution which Grattan and Flood had framed, and the First Irish Volunteers had secured; which already possessed historical and international status, and which needed no alteration, for the things which brought the Irish Parliament of 1782–1800 to the ground, were things which were not in the Constitution at all—the Lord Lieutenant and his control of patronage and his connexion with the English Privy Council. The Constitution included and contemplated none of these things; it specifically included the "King, Lords, and Commons of Ireland." And if we were to retain some connexion with England—and everybody agreed that we must since we could not beat her militarily—here was the connexion which would have been least irksome and most natural. There would have been no Partition, and the oath would have been an oath to the King of Ireland.

CHAPTER XVI.

THE GREAT TALK.

When the great talk began in the Dáil the stage had already been set for the tragedy which afterwards developed. Messrs. de Valera, Brugha, and Stack, had promulgated the myth of themselves as the innocents at home, trusting innocents, basely betrayed by Griffith and Collins; while Mr. Barton had promulgated that other myth of the Treaty having been signed under duress, under threat of immediate war. People were being called "Traitor"—that most bitter and ominous word in the Irish vocabulary. Bitterness bad arisen. Brugha and Mellowes were around the country, tampering with the Volunteers, having already made up their minds that whatever decision Dáil came to, the real decision would be made by the men with the guns. Mr. de Valera's poison-gas was working. He had let the bitterness loose. He had let the guns loose. He placed his whole moral force at the disposal of the men who were working to prevent a plebiscite, to prevent any sort of a vote on the Treaty, and who were prepared to go any lengths against it. He was never afterwards able to call his dogs, the dogs of war, back after loosing them.

The country wanted the Treaty—overwhelmingly. If the plebiscite which Griffith had demanded in December had been taken, there would have been an almost unanimous vote in favour of the Treaty. If the Treaty had been recommended to Dáil and to the country by the whole Cabinet—and as the whole Cabinet were responsible for it, they were in honour bound to recommend it—there would have been growls, but no effective opposition. There would have been no bitterness and no civil war. Mr. de Valera's treachery it was which turned victory into Dead Sea fruit, which made the bitterness and the civil war.

Into the great talk in the Dáil, and the great talk in the country, and the formation of the Anti-Treaty Party, there went more hypocrisy, lying, and moral cowardice than one would have believed to have existed in this country. The opposition to the Treaty in the Dáil was wholly dishonest. It had been made plain to the Deputies by Mr. de Valera, in public session and in private session, that they were negotiating for terms, and that he himself would not be bound rigidly by the oath to the Republic. They had before them, when they finally agreed to send plenipotentiaries to discuss terms, Mr. de Valera's own letters to Lloyd George, in which he was obviously bluffing in order to save his face, in which every time he went a bit too far he immediately wriggled, and in which he mentions the word Republic only to assure Mr. Lloyd George that he was not asking England to recognise it. They knew, every one of them, what was going to be done, and not one of them dared to oppose it effectively or to expose it; because there was not one of them who did not know then, that the Truce came only just in the nick of time—that the war, if it had gone on any longer, might have ended in a complete collapse; and because there was not one of them that would take the responsibility of breaking off the Truce or refusing the negotiations. The time to overthrow the Treaty was *before* it had been signed—when it was merely threatened. The time to vote against it was at the meetings of Dáil after the Lloyd George letter. Those who heard, there, Mr. de Valera's explanations, his threat to resign if he were bound to his oath, knew perfectly well they were abandoning the Republic. And those who did not vote against the Treaty then, before it was signed, had no right to vote against it after it was signed. The whole Dáil was responsible for the Treaty, and should have accepted its responsibility. It should not have put the responsibility on the country. But its members were not thinking of the country, but of their own little reputations. They wanted the Treaty to pass, but they wanted somebody else to vote for it. Men and women of the Dáil who had thrown up their hats in the air for the Treaty on that first morning decided, after Mr. de Valera's pronouncement, that they could not afford to be less extreme than he; and so the split was made, made out of treachery and spite and moral cowardice. Many a man spoke in the Dáil against the Treaty, and yet prayed God nightly that it would be carried.

In the country, the split was made similarly, except that it was made more honestly. There were some people, outside the ranks of Dáil, who did not believe the evidence of their senses; who did believe that the Truce and the negotiations meant nothing but a trick on the English; who never dreamed that the Dáil Cabinet, or Dáil itself, would ever consider any arrangement but independence; and who did honestly and out of conviction oppose the Treaty. But the mass of the opposition, so far as it consisted of the opposition of people who had been active in the movement, was as dishonest as the mass of the opposition in Dáil. It consisted of people who saw the evidence of compromise but shut their eyes to it, and then, when the inevitable happened, attempted to "wrap the green flag round me." Outside those who had been in the movement, the opposition came from people who had not, but who now wished they had, and who discovered in the split a glorious opportunity of posing as extreme, of becoming heroes without any danger, for at this stage nobody anticipated what was going to happen.

All of that was exacerbated by the Great Talk, in which men got up day after day and talked for their reputations. In the course of it, I met an Anti-Treaty T.D. whom I had known well in London. "People outside think," said he to me, "that this is a question of the Republic against the Treaty. It is not. It is a question of the Treaty against Document No. 2, and there isn't a particle of difference between them." Yet he voted for Document No. 2.

For my part, if England agreed to accept either the Treaty or Document No. 2, I would vote for the Treaty. Between the two there is no substantial difference in fact, but an immense difference in implication. The Treaty is an arrangement forced upon us by England and binding us in honour only so long as we are unable to renounce it. No Treaty is binding in perpetuity or in all circumstances. It is not a final settlement, nor has it been accepted as a final settlement. Document No. 2, on the other hand, was our proposal, put forward by our plenipotentiaries as a settlement. If accepted, it would have bound us in honour not to enlarge it.

In this connexion, I may set down here a conversation which I had with Griffith in April, 1922. I had to see him in connexion with Post Office business, and when that was finished, I put to him a question which I had been wanting an opportunity to put. [I had seen him only once since his release from prison, and then in a crowd.] I said to him, "How did 'external association' first arise?" "I'll tell you," said he. "The first I heard of 'external association' was when Dev was pressing me to go over as plenipotentiary. I went into him one day, and found him with Cathal and Austin at his desk, all three sitting. I was standing. He told me he wanted me to go to London. I said to him, 'You are my chief, and if you tell me to go, I'll go. But I know, and you know, that I can't bring back the Republic.' Then he produced this *external association* idea—the first I ever heard of it—and after half-an-hour's persuasion, Cathal gave a reluctant consent to it. Stack said nothing, but sat there, sullen. I said nothing. Then the other two left, and left me alone with him. I said to him, Look here, Dev, what is the meaning of this *external association* idea? What are you getting at with it?' He replied by getting a pencil and paper and drawing a straight line thus—[Here Griffith got pencil and paper and drew the line AB]—'That,' said he, 'is me, in the

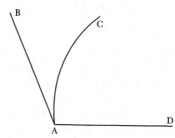

straight jacket of the Republic. I must get out of it.' Then he drew another line, a curved line. [Here Griffith drew the curved line AC]. 'That,' said he, 'is external association. The purpose of it is to bring Cathal along.' Then he drew another straight line—[Here Griffith drew the line AD]—'That,' said he, 'is where we'll eventually get to.' Then I was satisfied, and said no more about it."

I believe that statement of Griffith's, given in private and friendly conversation, to have been absolutely truthful, and to fit in with everything we know of Mr. de Valera. He never had any illusions about Ireland's chances of getting a Republic, and when he first nailed the Republican flag to his masthead, he was only nailing a flag for political and bargaining purposes— he was not nailing a principle. The idea of compromise was ever present with him, and he was the first Irishman to suggest compromise, as he did in the journalistic interview in which he invited England to offer Ireland a Cuban Constitution. When he returned to Ireland in December, 1920, his first thought was to stop the war, the growing brutality of which, he perceived, made any arrangement difficult.

The Great Talk, at any rate, revealed nothing but bitterness and 'jealousy and small-mindedness in the members of Dáil. They spoke, not on the subject at issue, but to posterity— thinking of their reputations, and not of their responsibilities nor of the consequences of their words or acts. Men and women who had looked on and watched the Republic being thrown overboard, pretended they wanted to die for it when the irrevocable deed had been done. The whole debate was an exposure of the vanity and incompetence of Dáil members, and of their political irresponsibility. The question at issue was a simple one and a clear one, yet numbers of the Deputies changed their minds day after day, swayed by this or by that. On the last day of all, one Deputy, at least, voted against the Treaty because the *Freeman's Journal* had attacked de Valera; while at least two others voted in its favour because of a bitter speech by Cathal Brugha against Collins. The Plenipotentiaries themselves furnished the crowning evidence of our utter absence of any sense of responsibility, inasmuch as one plenipotentiary, who did not like the Treaty after he had signed it, regarded himself as at liberty to dishonour his signature and vote and act with the Anti-Treaty Party; while another, who honoured his signature in the letter, completely broke it in the spirit, and gave every encouragement, short of joining them, to those who worked for the rejection of the Treaty.

The debate revealed the mass of the Deputies engulfed in moral cowardice and in rhetoric, desperately attempting to save their faces either by pretending to believe that they were voting for the "maintenance of the existing Republic" while they were really voting for Document No. 2, or by pretending to believe that they were voting for a future Republic, when they were really voting for the postponement of the Republican demand. The machine which Sinn Féin had become produced what political machines always produce—mediocrity and codology and political incapacity.

CHAPTER XVII.

THE POSITION CREATED BY THE TRUCE
AND THE TREATY.

The issue as between the Treaty and the Anti-Treaty Parties has been so befogged and muddled by the side issues and passions of the Great Talk, and by what followed, that it may not be inopportune here to set down the actual position in which Ireland was placed by the Truce and the Treaty.

The Election of 1918 placed the authority of the Irish people in the hands of Sinn Féin. That did not mean that the Irish people were irrevocably pledged to the Sinn Féin programme and policy; but it did mean that they agreed that that programme and policy afforded then the most hopeful avenues of approach to the achievement of Irish freedom. It meant that Ireland trusted Sinn Féin to get independence if it could, but especially to do its best for the people in any given circumstances—Mr. de Valera's interpretation of the Republican oath being not alone the true interpretation of that oath, but also the true interpretation of the vote which the people gave at both the Sinn Féin General Elections.

Sinn Féin itself knew all the time during the struggle that its power to hold Ireland depended largely on England not tempting Ireland with a reasonable offer of settlement. It knew that while Ireland as a whole, for the first time for over two centuries, supported a separatist programme, it did so as an ultimate principle and not an immediate achievement; and that, while it would go to great lengths in order to achieve now that ultimate principle, it would not refuse to go on with any reasonable settlement short of that, which it could use towards that ultimate principle. Adhesion to Sinn Féin in 1918 no

more committed Ireland to consider nothing but independence than adhesion to Parnell in 1885 committed Ireland to
consider nothing but Home Rule. "There are but two great
parties in the end," those who are for Ireland and those who
are against Ireland; and the victory at the polls of any one of
the parties who make up the right one of the two great parties
meant nothing more than that Ireland asked that party to
wield its authority and to do its best for Ireland on its own
particular policy and programme.

It was obvious, after the turning down of Ireland by the
Versailles Peace Conference and the United States of America,
that independence was not feasible. It could not be won by
physical force, because we had not, nor could we possibly
develop, enough physical force to balance England's physical
force. It could not be won by diplomacy and international
intrigue, because the only Great Power which might be
expected to support Ireland had definitely turned Ireland
down and would do nothing to force England to agree to
independence; and because none of the smaller powers who
might have liked to support us dare do it, with England stronger
than ever she had been. The war, which had impoverished
Europe, had made it cynical, and weakened tremendously its
sympathy with small nations. The nations that had won the
war were engaged in carving slices out of those which had lost,
against all decency and justice; while the nations that had lost
the war were too concerned about their own amputated limbs
to care a damn what happened to us. We had no longer an
international hearing which could be of any use to us, outside
of England itself. If independence was to come, it could only
come by agreement with England. If England lacked the will
to that agreement, we could not force her to agree—and no
other nation was likely to.

In these circumstances, the duty of Sinn Féin was not to its
own party or to its own particular principle, but to the nation
as a whole. Its business was to do its best for the nation in
whatever circumstances might arise. Independence was not
feasible in the circumstances. Mr. de Valera knew that, as his
every action showed. Mr. Griffith knew that. Mr. Collins

knew that. Cathal Brugha knew that—as his acceptance of "external association," Document No. 2, Mr. de Valera's "form of oath," and a yearly tribute to King George, showed. They all knew it, but they pretended that they did not.

The Truce came at a time when the people were getting tired of the war, tired especially of the disregard shown by the Volunteers for the ordinary citizen, and when operations were getting more difficult and arms and ammunition scarce. The Black-and-Tan tyranny, though it was a fleabite compared to the Irregular tyranny which followed it, was so much in advance of anything we had known or heard of since '98 that it seemed to us the last refinement of frightfulness, and the people as a whole would have taken any reasonable settlement to get rid of the war and the "Tans." The Truce created peace conditions and intensified the already existing will to peace. It demoralised the Volunteers (drink) in large areas. It increased their numbers hut hardly their *morale*. It made a renewal of the fight with any hope of success or general popular support impossible, unless it were renewed on a refusal by England to agree to a settlement which could be accepted. The longer the Truce went on, the more impossible it became to refuse any terms which might be offered, and which were not absolutely impossible.

The Treaty, when it came, offered Ireland a settlement which the majority of the people considered reasonable, which they thought could be accepted and should be accepted. There was no doubt about that at the time, and there is no doubt about it now. Had Dáil Eireann rejected the Treaty it would not have reflected Irish opinion, any more than did Foster's Parliament when it passed the Union in 1800.

That being the position what ought Sinn Féin to have done?

There were two courses open to it. The first was to say "We cannot decide this as a Party question; we have to do our best for the people as a whole. The people trusted us, and we are their servants. We cannot at present get independence, but we can get this Treaty, and the people as a whole want the Treaty given a chance. We knew in our hearts in July last that the Truce and the negotiations meant a compromise. Let us, then, take the responsibility which is properly ours; let us ratify this Treaty, and let us use it in order to enable ourselves at some future date, or our successors, to take the final step of separation."

The second way was to say, "This Dáil is a *war* Dáil and not a peace Dáil. It does not really represent the nation; it does not really represent even the best of Sinn Féin. The whole circumstances of its formation and its personnel make it a body not competent to settle this question of itself. The people as a whole are entitled to be heard. We will go to them and say: 'You gave us a mandate to secure independence. We have tried—in blood and suffering. We have not succeeded. We are offered this, which is less than independence, but which is more than anybody ten years ago deemed possible of achievement. We ask you to pronounce upon it.'"

It was Sinn Féin's test, and it failed the test. It adopted neither of the statesmanlike and sensible courses which were open to it, and it blundered terribly by considering the whole question from a narrow Party and personal point of view. The Great Talk gave no consideration to what the nation wanted, or to what was best for the nation, but to ephemeral things like "What did A say to B on the xth day of y?" to considerations of personal vanity and reputation. Instead of considering whether the country should ratify the Treaty, they considered: "Can Sinn Féin afford to accept the Treaty? Can *I* afford to vote for it?" They should have put both Party and self out of consideration, for once a tangible proposition had come out of their work, neither was proper to be considered. The result of the muddle in thought, muddle in leadership, was that many voted against the Treaty who wanted the Treaty to pass, who wanted to vote for it, but were afraid—afraid for their Party, afraid for themselves, afraid for their oath. In the course of the Great Talk, Liam Mellowes, in admitting that the people wanted the Treaty, said that it was the people's fear that urged them. The contrary was the case. It was fear, moral fear, lack of moral courage, which was responsible for most of the votes cast against the Treaty; and the votes cast for it were the votes of those who had at least partly conquered fear, who had put themselves and their strict Party principles aside, and remembered the nation; who recognised that they had led Ireland into a mess, and that they had to take their responsibilities; and who voted despite the threats of assassination and of war, which were freely made almost from the day when Mr. de Valera gave the signal for the split.

Sinn Féin should, I think, have followed the second of the courses referred to above. It should have accompanied that by the abandonment of the dominance which it had obtained for its own organisation, have given a fair field, and have gone to the polls as an ordinary Party on a programme of separation, to be attained by the use of the Treaty in the ordinary way for the furtherance of separation. That, of course, was Collins' policy, but it did not get a chance.

CHAPTER XVIII.

THE PSEUDO-REPUBLICANS.

The ratification of the Treaty by Dáil Eireann was followed by the formation, by Mr. de Valera and his friends, of themselves into a Party which eventually called itself the Republican Party. Its original quarrel with the majority was not on the Republic, but on Document No. 2; but as Document No. 2 was discovered to be incapable of maintaining or extending a Party, it was dropped, and the Republic substituted. Mr. de Valera, however, remained faithful to Document No. 2, and has at various times declared that he stands by it—but nobody else does. The particular lie upon which the new Party was founded, and upon which it still stands, is the lie that its members, or rather its founders—the fifty-seven Deputies who voted against the Treaty—were noble heroes who never agreed to any modification of the demand for independence; who never knew, in the period between the Truce and the Treaty, that there was any question of such a modification; and who never faltered in their determination to, as the cant has it, "maintain the existing Republic."

Now, the said Deputies were told by Mr. de Valera, before the plenipotentiaries were appointed, not brutally and directly but delicately and indirectly, that there was going to be a compromise, and any pretence that they did not know it is a lie. The most average intelligence had only to devote five minutes' thought to the circumstances of the Truce, and the de Valera-Lloyd George correspondence, to see that the negotiations would be on the implicit basis of "No Republic," and that de Valera was merely trying to save his face. Furthermore, the issue on which the Dáil was divided was not on the Treaty *versus* the Republic, but on the Treaty *versus* Document No. 2; and those who voted against the Treaty voted for Document No. 2, and not for the Republic.

These Deputies, in fact, were those who had watched, during the summer and winter of 1921, the Republic being thrown overboard; and then, when an irrevocable step had been taken, had been seduced, either by Mr. de Valera or by their own moral cowardice, into the public hypocrisy which they have since maintained. Some of them just followed Mr. de Valera or Cathal Brugha; some of them just had not the courage to be honest; and some of them thought, after the Treaty was signed, that, after all, the Truce was a mistake, and it would be better to go back to war than to ratify the Treaty. All of them forgot the black outlook out of which the Truce came; all of them forgot the relief with which they themselves, and the country, greeted it; all of them had allowed themselves to be affected by the post-war bellicosity which had grown up during the long negotiations; and none of them were honest enough to give precisely their reasons; they all pretended to be standing on the high heroic principle of "No Compromise." They had, and have, no right whatever to call themselves Republicans. They are only pseudo-Republicans.

They were joined by a mixed gathering. Some honest people who really had been bewildered, and had not realised what was going on, and who were and are good separatists; and a vast host of cods of all sorts. All the people who had stood coldly on the outskirts of the "Tan" war, giving a frigid adhesion to Sinn Féin, but condemning in private everything which Sinn Féin did; all the people who had been apathetic during the "Tan" war, and had been seized, on the appearance of the Truce, with envy of those who had been active and who could talk about this and that "stunt," about "forty-fives," and "three-o-threes" and T.N.T.; all the people who had refused to shelter Volunteers and afterwards wished they had not refused—they all joined the pseudo-Republicans and went about in a blaze of glory, wrapping the green flag around them. They never meant to do anything but pose, and the majority of them have never done anything but pose; and if they could have known at the beginning that they were making civil war, they would have remained in their accustomed ease; but, just as Mr. de Valera had not the moral courage to attempt to control the evil which he let loose—although he condemned it privately—so these rank-and-filers of his were led by weakness and cowardice into responsibility for the foulnesses which shamed Ireland in the civil war.

It is a dangerous thing to play with human passions and to appeal to mob law. Sir Edward Carson, who talked guns against the English without meaning it, and organised Volunteers as an election bluff, loosed forces which he could not control, and is—in a sense—responsible for Easter Week and the "Tan" war; while Mr. de Valera, who threatened civil war against Griffith and Collins without meaning it, also loosed forces which he could not control, and is responsible for all the blood and bitterness of the civil war.

At any rate, the "Republican" movement which was founded after the ratification of the Treaty, was founded on a lie and is maintained on a lie. Its policy has been a policy of attack on the Irish people. It has neither patriotism nor decency. It has shamed the name Republic and made it stink. It has weakened Ireland economically, morally, and internationally, and it has appreciably delayed the establishment of complete independence. It stressed the things in the Treaty which are irksome to all Irishmen; and, by drawing England's attention to these things, by making test questions of them, it has prevented any modification of them. They will all go eventually—the oath and the Governor-General and the Privy Council and Partition. But some of them would have gone ere this were it not for the pseudo-Republicans, and all of them will now be somewhat overdue when they depart.

The oath and the other things were put in the Treaty, not because they have or were meant to have any practical relation to Irish government, but because it was necessary to put in the Treaty certain things to save England's face. That was all England wanted. When Mr. Childers and Mr. de Valera and Miss MacSwiney and the other blind leaders of the blind made the welkin ring with them; when they made test questions of them, when they spent a whole Dáil Session fulminating about them, they made it impossible to modify them.

CHAPTER XIX.

THE FURIES.

"Hell hath no fury like a woman . . ."

I have already referred to the effect which the war had upon the women who were connected with the Volunteers. The long period of the Truce had upon them an effect even more deplorable than that which it had upon the Volunteers. They took not to drink, but to war. All the swashbuckling and bombast and swagger which were encouraged by the leaders after the Truce for the sake of keeping up the public spirit, went to their heads and they became more drunken than if they had consumed the strongest wine. Immediately the Truce came, they thought of nothing but war, and prepared for nothing but war. They took to splints, bandages, first-aid, drill, and guns, and thought of nothing else. To them the Truce was nothing but a trick played upon the British, and to them peace was a loveless thing, and no life so good as the life of war. They became practically unsexed, their mother's milk blackened to make gunpowder, their minds working on nothing save hate and blood.

To the gunwoman the Truce was an irritation and the Treaty a calamity. Yet even they would not have made trouble were it not for Mr. de Valera. I have already recorded how one of them shrugged her shoulders and resigned herself to it before Mr. de Valera let loose anarchy; but when he called to the demons of bitterness and blood the gunwomen answered him joyfully and fiercely. They wanted war, and the excitement of war, and the irresponsibility and destruction and freedom of war, and they went more wholeheartedly and more fiercely into the war against the Irish people than ever they had into the war against the Black-and-Tans.

Of the women members of Dáil who voted against the Treaty, I deal separately with Miss Mary MacSwiney. Countess Markievicz, Mrs. O'Callaghan, Mrs. Pearse, and Dr. Ada English were at first rather in favour of the Treaty than against it, but became Anti-Treaty because the strength of Mr. de Valera's "betrayal" current carried them away. Dr. Ada English's particular reason for voting anti-Treaty deserves, however, to be specially recorded. She came up from Galway to vote for a settlement, but when she arrived she said, "All the women should stand together," and so she voted with the others—not because she thought they were right, but because they were a sex. Her vote was a sex vote. Mrs. Clarke was one of the very few Deputies who never had, and never pretended to have, any illusions as to what the Truce meant, and her vote against the Treaty was because she disliked it, and not because of Mr. de Valera's "betrayal" pose.

Having taken sides, the women at once proceeded to worsen the situation. It was a woman who said, before ever the Treaty vote was taken, "If no man be found to shoot Mick Collins, I'll shoot him myself"; and it is women who were largely responsible for the bitterness and the ferocity of the civil war. In the whole period of war, both the "Tan" war and the civil war, the women were the implacable and irrational upholders of death and destruction. They never understood the political situation and they never tried to understand it—not indeed that the majority of the men were any better in that respect—but the women jumped to conclusions without any consideration whatever, save their emotions, and once having done so, never afterwards looked facts in the face or attempted a re-examination of the situation. Their influence, even in the "Tan" war, was not good, but in the civil war it was wholly bad.

Left to himself, man is comparatively harmless. He will always exchange smokes and drinks and jokes with his enemy, and he will always pity the "poor devil" and wish that the whole business was over. The thought of his parents, or of his wife or his children, is always with him to make him consider a friendly arrangement rather than a duel, to make him think of life rather than of death. He will throw aside his passions and his feelings in deference to that social instinct in him which has made civilisation to advance by training him to count the cost.

It is woman, woman adrift with her white feathers or whatever else fulfils in other conditions the same purpose, with her implacability, her bitterness, her hysteria, that makes a devil of him. The Suffragettes used to tell us that with women in political power there would be no more war. We know better now. We know that with women in political power there would be no more peace.

CHAPTER XX.

MARY MACSWINEY—"SEA-GREEN INCORRUPTIBLE."

Of all the impostures with which the Anti-Treaty Party is made up, perhaps the most shameless and loathsome (after that of de Valera) is that which Miss Mary MacSwiney has so persistently and sedulously foisted on the country—the imposture of herself as a "Sea-green Incorruptible."

Miss MacSwiney knew, before the plenipotentiaries were appointed, that the Republic had been thrown overboard; she knew, when she was going to the Session of Dáil which appointed the plenipotentiaries, that she was going to agree to the appointment of plenipotentiaries who would not discuss a Republic.

Miss MacSwiney was in America when the Truce was signed. About ten days afterwards, I had a letter from Miss Annie MacSwiney, asking me what it meant, and saying that they were very uneasy about it in Cork. I replied that I had no inside knowledge of any kind, but that to anybody with any political intelligence it was plain that the Republic had been abandoned and that we were going to negotiate for the best terms we could get. This opinion was passed on to Miss Mary MacSwiney. I was away when she returned from America, but a couple of days after my return to business she came to see me, and the following conversation ensued:—

"Well, Mary, you see I was right." (It was then the beginning of September, 1921, and I did not conceive that anybody could possibly then have any doubts about what was happening).

"No, I don't admit that, yet."

"Why not?"

"Well, I've been to see de Valera, and I asked him was he compromising, and he assures me that he stands where he always stood."

"Very well, Mary. Now, leave de Valera out of it and use your own intelligence. De Valera spent a week with Lloyd George, in private conclave. Nobody knows what they discussed. But do you think they discussed a Republic?"

"Well, no; I don't."

"Very well. Now you are going to a Dáil meeting to appoint delegates to a conference with English delegates. Do you think they are going to discuss a Republic?"

"Well, no; I don't."

"Then what the devil do you mean by pretending that I was not right?"

"I know we won't get a Republic, but I think we might get some semi-independent connexion with England which we could accept."

That, which conceded my point, ended the conversation. And it is all I have to say with regard to Miss Mary MacSwiney's "Sea-green Incorruptible" pose, and her pretence that she is a better Republican than Mick Collins or than any of the Republicans who were shot by her fellow pseudo-Republicans in the civil war.

To the whole split and civil war, Miss MacSwiney contributed nothing but bitterness and hatred and malignancy. From the beginning of the split, she worked to create bitterness, and her influence has always been fatal. On the night the vote was taken, I heard Mick Collins, after the vote, make an appeal to the other side to co-operate with him in keeping peace and order in Ireland. I have always believed that if Mr. de Valera had answered that appeal, he would have answered it in the spirit in which it was made; but he did not get the opportunity. Before he or anybody else could draw a breath, Miss MacSwiney was on her feet, hatred and passion in her face and in her voice. "No," said she, "we will not co-operate with you nor help you in any way. You are worse than Castlereagh." She had only one policy then, and she has only one policy now; and she committed her party to it then, and that is—to make trouble for the Government of the Irish people, in the name of that Republic which she and her friends have shamed and dishonoured.

CHAPTER XXI.

AFTER THE RATIFICATION.

The situation created by the ratification of the Treaty was a curious and an alarming one. In the first place, Mr. de Valera and the pseudo-Republicans began to regret that they had allowed the thing to come to a vote at all, and cast about for some means of undoing that vote. They found it in Mr. de Valera's melodramatic resignation of the Presidency of Dáil and his dishonest attempt, immediately afterwards, to get himself re-elected. Upon the defeat of that attempt, they abandoned all thought of votes, and fell back upon threats and upon muddling the public mind by talk about "the existing Republic" and the "Government of the Republic" and the "Army of the Republic"; by which they sought to convey, and succeeded in conveying to the people, that they were all "Sea-green Incorruptibles," while those who voted for the Treaty and tried to give it a chance were "traitors" and "scum." And they were enabled to do that because of the extraordinary way in which both Griffith and Collins accepted their false premises and made no attempt to put the facts of the new situation plainly before the people.

In the course of the Great Talk there was no real attempt to be frank, and both sides talked about the Republic and the army of the Republic and about the maintenance of the Government of the Republic. When Dáil, on January 7th, 1922, ratified the Treaty, it was comparatively easy then for the pseudo-Republicans to ensure the carrying on of a Dáil Government, as distinct from the Provisional Government. But that was illegal and grotesque. When Dáil Eireann ratified the

Treaty on the 7th January, it automatically dropped the Republic, and changed its own basis. It had no longer the right to function as a Republican Dáil, or as anything else but the Dáil which would represent the people under the new political status established by the Treaty. Dáil Eireann had, in accordance with the wishes of the Irish people, accepted the Treaty, accepted for Ireland a status which was less than independence, and as a Republican Dáil it was thenceforward dead. Nor did any moral nor constitutional right remain in the Anti-Treaty minority to form themselves into a Republican Dáil. They had the right, and the duty, to form a Party, and to form it upon Republican principles; but they had no fight to form a government, or to speak or act in the name of the Irish people, because they represented neither the people nor the Dáil which the people had last elected. They represented nobody but themselves.

After the Treaty vote was taken, Dáil should have dissolved *sine die.* Its work was done. It had represented the people, and it had won for the people something which the people wished to be put into operation as an experiment. Not one of the sixty-four Members who voted for the Treaty did so because he liked it, or because he was satisfied with it, but because the people wanted it and because in the circumstances there was no honourable alternative to it. Having done the people's work, there was nothing more for them to do. The future of Ireland should have been left to a new assembly to be elected in the new state of things. Those who had been elected as separatists and who found themselves obliged to ratify something which was less than separation, should have gone to the country at once and explained why and how, and should have sought re-election, if at all, on the definite basis of working the Treaty. They had no right whatever to give any countenance to the solemn and mischievous farce of "maintaining the existing Republic" after that Republic had been turned down after a month's debate by the representatives of the people in accordance with the will of the people. But when a Dáil Cabinet, as distinct from the Provisional Government, was maintained, when Griffith in becoming President of Dáil in succession to Mr. de Valera, agreed, by implication, that he was "President of the Government of the Republic," and when Dick Mulcahy, in taking over the Ministry of Defence, declared that "the army will remain the army of the Irish Republic," nobody knew where anybody was. That attitude only encouraged the pseudo-Republicans and strengthened their following.

The position was, of course, not an easy one. The pseudo-Republicans knew that they stood no chance on either a plebiscite or a general election, and they put every possible hindrance in the way of any appeal to the people. In so far as they had a constitutional policy then, it was that there should be no appeal to the country until such time as they were certain of a majority, and that, in the meantime, there should be a Gilbertian Dáil-Provisional Government, as a sort of Spenlow and Jorkins arrangement. And they prepared to get their majority by a propagandist campaign of unexampled hypocrisy and mendacity, and by raising that most potent epithet of all epithets in Ireland—"Traitor!"

But, allowing for all the difficulties with which Collins and Griffith were confronted, the situation was completely mishandled. In the first instance, by the acquiescence in the maintenance of two Governments; and in the second place, by the failure to keep the public informed of what was happening. As early as January, 1922, Collins knew that the Irregulars were arming and organising, and knew that they meant to strike at the Provisional Government. If he had then and in the subsequent months taken the public into his confidence, if he had then and in the subsequent months forced the pseudo-Republicans to come out into the Open, if he had exposed their hypocrisy—Mr. de Valera in one room at 23 Suffolk Street, waxing dithyrambic about the allegiance everybody owed to Dáil, and Mr. Rory O'Connor in the adjoining room dictating to journalists declarations of war against Dáil—the Irregular movement would have been circumscribed by the force of public opinion within limits which would have minimised its power to do harm. But he was too obsessed with the idea of not letting the public know, too confident that a secret bridge could be built and maintained between those who were the servants of the Irish people and those who wanted to be their masters.

CHAPTER XXII.

THE IRREGULARS.

Side by side with the attempts to maintain a "Government of the Republic" side by side with the Provisional Government, went the attempt to maintain the army as a Republican army. To that attempt countenance was given by Dick Mulcahy when he guaranteed that it should remain "the army of the Republic," even though he only meant that to stand during the transition period between the ratification or the Treaty and the definite establishment of the Free State contemplated by it. But the Anti-Treaty Party put no limits to its duration and, realising that they had no chance of beating the Treaty by votes, they determined to beat it by force.

From the first day of the split, everybody saw that much would depend on what the Volunteers did. If they behaved as the servants of the Irish people and accepted the decision of Dáil, if they acted in truth as the army of the people and not the army of a Party, then all would be well; and if not, not. If they had been let alone they would have acted as the army of the people and would not have interfered in politics. The rank and file of them did not want to touch politics, and if they had been given the chance of holding together as the army of the people, to do the people's will and safeguard the people's decrees, they would gladly have done that and left political decisions to the politicians. But they were not given the chance. The pseudo-Republicans, knowing that they were in a decided minority in the country, determined to use the army in order to hold up the Treaty, and organised with that purpose. Certain of the politicians had, even before the Treaty vote was taken, gone around the country tampering with various units; and in January, 1922, Rory O'Connor, Ernie O'Malley, and Oscar Traynor formed a secret G.H.Q. in Dublin, and started to organise within the army, to store arms, et cetera— an exact replica of the situation immediately preceding the Rising of 1916, except that the secret G.H.Q. of 1916 was preparing an attack upon Ireland's enemy, whereas the secret G.H.Q. of 1922 was preparing an attack upon Ireland herself.

The seed that the man with the gun was a law unto himself, and that the mere civilian did not count, did not fall upon stony ground. The whole later course of the "Tan" war prepared a fruitful field for it. Over large tracts of country the local Volunteer Commandant was supreme; and after the Truce in particular, when he was supreme publicly instead of secretly, when he was both soldier and policeman, when men who had never fired a shot found themselves possessed with power, the pride and truculence of the gunman grew. They were told, and then they told each other, that they had beaten England, that they had won the war; and then, when the Treaty came, they were told that it was they, who had beaten England and won the war, who should decide whether the Treaty should be accepted or not; and they were further told that of course they, who had beaten England, who had sworn an oath to the Republic, would never agree to a Treaty which gave Ireland less than a Republic. And being for the most part young and inexperienced, they were as clay in the hands of the politicians and intriguers, who played with men's lives in order to save their own faces.

Rory O'Connor's G.H.Q. came into the open in due course, making its debut from Mr. de Valera's headquarters at 23 Suffolk Street, while he himself pretended to know nothing about it and to have no connexion with it. It proceeded, through mutiny and secession, to a "Convention" which elected an executive to control the irregular army it had created, and declared that there was no need to worry about money as "there was plenty in Banks and Post Offices"; and it proceeded thence to the robbery of buildings in which to house its army, of goods to feed and clothe it, and of money to pay it. "The Irish people will pay," said Rory O'Connor lightly, when asked where some unfortunate despoiled individual would get his money. *They have paid.*

As early as January, 1922, Collins knew of the preparations which were being made to strike at the Provisional Government. "They can only be preparing to strike at us," said he; "there is nobody else for them to strike at." The only effective action which he could have taken—to have exposed the whole business then at the beginning, appealed to the people for support against the setting up of a military tyranny and thus force Mr. de Valera to show his hand—he did not take. He had nothing left then but to build up an army of his own, and build it up so strongly that its strength would deter his opponents from any attack, other than constitutional, on the Treaty position.

Given the situation as it was in Ireland, the Irregulars were an inevitable consequence of the play-acting of the pseudo-Republicans. Most of the latter gentry, when they began, had no purpose other than to pose—visualising themselves as picturesque, extreme, soulful, non-compromisers, shouting defiance at the Free State, but very happy in their own minds that the Free State was there—and being sentimentally maudlin over their several glasses of grog. The whole evolution was an extraordinary example of the power of words. These people played with words and their words took form and plagued them. They talked guns, and their rhetoric was translated into weapons by the realists. They preached that "the people had no right to go wrong"—to go wrong being to vote against Mr. de Valera—and the realists at once said "To hell with the people." They preached that the Dáil had no right to ratify the Treaty because it was elected to get the Republic, and the realists at once said "To hell with the Dáil." They called Griffith, Collins, Mulcahy, and the rest "Traitor!" and the realists at once said, "The penalty of treason is death." Until, at the end of all, Liam Lynch issued a solemn proclamation dividing up the "enemy"—the Irregular name for the Irish people—into some dozen different categories, all of whom were to be eliminated.

So much mischief from the moral cowardice of one man! For Mr. de Valera was solely responsible for the pseudo-Republicans and for the Irregulars.

CHAPTER XXIII.

DEVIL ERA.

"If they accepted the Treaty, and if the Volunteers of the future tried to complete the work the Volunteers of the last four years had been attempting, they would have to complete it, not over the bodies of foreign soldiers, but over the dead bodies of their own countrymen.

"They would have to wade through Irish blood, through the blood of the soldiers of the Irish Government, and through, perhaps, the blood of some of the members of the Government, in order to get Irish freedom,"

—*Mr. de Valera's Message to Ireland on St. Patrick's Day, 1922.*

The fruits of the Great Talk, of the secret G.H.Q., and of the lying pseudo-Republican propaganda were not long in appearing. First, there was a bitterness more intense and more murderous than any that has been in Ireland within living memory; old friendships went for nought, family ties went for nought, hatred and thoughts of murder stalked the land. Then there were attacks upon British forces leaving, or preparing to leave, the country; raids for arms; attacks upon retired R.I.C. men in various places; attacks upon Protestants; finally attacks upon Volunteers who were standing by the decision of Dáil Eireann. The twenty-six counties became a huge armed camp with, in most towns, armed men glaring at each other from opposite sides of the street; with the secret G.H.Q. becoming more and more bent upon business; with no police force and no public confidence. On St. Patrick's Day, 1922, Mr. de Valera made the pronouncement above quoted to an inflammable country audience; and on the 19th he repeated it in substance to another country audience. Messrs. Brugha and MacEntee at the same time delivered themselves of pronouncements of the same nature. Evidently the pseudo-Republicans had taken a decision.

The effect was electrical. Mr. de Valera's gunmen had now received his blessing, and they were free from any doubt as to how far he was prepared to go. All the irresponsibles, all the slanderers, all the poison tongues, all the uprooters, who had gathered round the Great Anarch were now loosed and spurred on, and through Ireland they went like so many devils, doing the devil's work everywhere. The secret G.H.Q. came out into the open with a furore, occupied the Four Courts, split the army, declared "To hell with Dáil," robbed goods and cash, started to do "stunts" against the army in Dublin, and joyfully made ready to wade through Irish blood when Mr. de Valera should require it.

CHAPTER XXIV.

THE WAR AGAINST THE IRISH PEOPLE.

> *" . . . That we do teach*
> *Bloody instructions which, being taught, return*
> *To plague the inventor."*

The proximate cause of the civil war which devastated Ireland in 1922–23, was the arrest by the Irregulars of General O'Connell of the National Army. Its real cause must be sought much earlier than that; it was in the insistence of the pseudo-Republicans that there must be no democratic appeal to the people on the Treaty issue; in their repeated declarations that a minority had the right to compel a majority if it could; in their threats of civil war and their preparations for civil war. So long as they set up the bullet against the ballot, as they did, civil war was inevitable, and the O'Connell affair was only the accidental cause.

Immediately the Treaty controversy started, the pseudo-Republicans recognised that they were in a very substantial minority. At first they were confident that Dáil would reject the Treaty, and when the final vote was taken Mr. de Valera could not believe his ears. It was, even then, impossible to him that he should be beaten, and his mind refused to accept it. His bearing was that of a man utterly overwhelmed with surprise and chagrin. Beaten in Dáil, and knowing that they would be beaten in the country, they placed their reliance on the gun, on forcing the Provisional Government, by the threat of the gun, to withhold putting the Treaty into operation, or to put it into operation shorn of its objectionable features. But in order to maintain that threat effectively, they would have to prevent the Provisional Government from having any army or any police force. Therefore it was that they objected to any recruiting for the army, any establishment of a police force, in the months before the outbreak, when attempts to maintain a united Dáil were being made. And they seem to have believed that they did hold the majority of the army. It was only a short while before the outbreak that the Irregulars held a Volunteer Parade in Dublin at which Oscar Traynor declared that there would be no fighting because ninety-nine per cent. of the army was with them.

In connexion with the coming of the civil war, this may be the best place to set down a conversation I had with Griffith on the last occasion on which I saw him. I saw him in his own room, on the second day of the Four Courts fighting, and I was shocked at the change in him. Those who were in close touch with him in the months previous to that say that the strain upon him was terrific, and that he was visibly killing himself working. But on this particular day he was obviously sick unto death, sick in his soul. He sat there, brooding, now and again writing, with all his gaiety and humour gone from him, like a man waiting for some inevitable thing. After a while he addressed two short sentences at me rather than to me, without looking at me. "Of course, those fellows will assassinate myself and Collins." And then, after a pause "De Valera is responsible for this—for all of it. There would have been no trouble but for him." I said to him: "It was unfortunate that the attack should so nearly coincide with Churchill's speech." " Yes, it was," said he, "but it was a pure coincidence. When the garage was occupied, we nearly decided to move; but when O'Connell was kidnapped we did decide to move, and the order was given. Then came Churchill's speech, and we wavered again. Some of us wanted to cancel it. But we said that we had either to go on or to abdicate, and finally we went on." From another source, I had already known that the decision had been taken before Churchill's speech, and by a combined meeting of the Dáil Cabinet and the Provisional Government.

The course of the war speedily demonstrated the falsity of the Irregulars' position and calculations. They were on the defensive from the outset in Dublin and throughout most of the country, and they were in a great minority generally so far as popular support was concerned. They were gradually driven into occupying towards the National Army the relative position which the Irish Volunteers had occupied towards the British Army, with the exception that the British could not beat the Volunteers because these had the people with them; whereas the National Army, with the people with them, beat the Irregulars, who were, perhaps, ten times as numerous as the serving Volunteers at their period of greatest strength, and whose proud boast it was that they had many more men in arms against the Free State in Dublin alone than had been in arms in all Ireland against the British.

As they lost the war, the Irregulars grew savage. At first their operations were directed against the National Army, but they speedily extended them to the civilian supporters of the Free State. Civilians were shot out of hand for the crime of standing by the Government of the Irish people; their houses, business and private, were destroyed; roads and bridges were destroyed and re-destroyed; railway lines were destroyed, and railway stations and rolling stock; food and goods were destroyed; amusements were "proclaimed" and many attacks made on harmless picture-houses. There was unrestrained shooting and unrestrained looting and unrestrained robbery, and a general attack upon the whole social fabric.

The Irregulars, in fact, had speedily realised that they had no popular support, that the Irish people supported the Treaty and the Government established by it, that they themselves were the enemies of the people, and they accepted that position. Their attack was not on the National Army, but on the Irish People; it was carried out with the intention of making a wilderness where they could not rule, and stopped at nothing. They declared the Irish people to be outlaws in their own land, and they treated them as such. They were insolent, brutal, unpatriotic, bloody and barbarous. There is not a word of justification nor excuse to be said for them. Mr. de Valera, of course, condemned all this in private, but in public he cheered them on.

When the English invaded Ireland and started to "civilise" us, the Irish Church regarded it as a punishment because of our sins against the British in the matter of raids and slaves. But I know of no clearer example of the application of the Moral Law than this tragedy of the Irregular devastation of Ireland. We devised certain "bloody instructions" to use against the British. We adopted political assassination as a principle; we devised the ambush; we encouraged women to forget their sex and play at gunmen; we turned the whole thoughts and passions of a generation upon blood and revenge and death; we placed gunmen, mostly half-educated and totally inexperienced, as dictators with powers of life and death over large areas. We derided the Moral Law, and said there was no law but the law of force. And the Moral Law answered us. Every devilish thing we did against the British went its full circle and then boomeranged and smote us ten-fold; and the cumulative effect of the whole of it was a general moral weakening and a general degradation and a general cynicism and disbelief in either virtue or decency, in goodness or uprightness or honesty. The Irregulars drove patriotism and honesty and morality out of Ireland. They fouled all the wells which had kept us clean, and made the task of saving Ireland ten-fold harder than it had been. They made people ask themselves whether Ireland was worth saving, and whether it was worth any man's while to trouble his head about anything but himself. They demonstrated to us that our deep-rooted belief that there was something in us finer than, more spiritual than, anything in any other people, was sheer illusion, and that we were really an uncivilised people with savage instincts. And the shock of that plunge from the heights to the depths staggered the whole nation. The "Island of Saints and Scholars" is burst, like Humpty Dumpty, and we do not quite know yet what we are going to get in its place.

CHAPTER XXV.

THE DEATH OF GRIFFITH.

By the death of Arthur Griffith we lost not only the most constructive and steadfast political intelligence in Ireland, but the man upon whom for twenty and odd years had lain the whole burden of the travail of this nation, and upon whom by rights it should have lain for at least another ten. Arthur Griffith was not alone the greatest Irishman of his time, but he was the greatest Irishman since Davis and Mitchel, and perhaps the most gifted all-round nationalist since Tone.

I had gone away to get a brief holiday, when this fatal news reached me. I could not believe it. Nobody who had known Griffith and worked with him could believe it. I felt as Gavan Duffy records the Young Irelanders felt when Davis died. Whoever else died, we felt sure that it would not be Griffith—Griffith with the iron will, the iron constitution, the imperturbable nerve; Griffith whom we all thought certain to live to be one hundred and write the epitaphs of all of us; Griffith, upon whom we all leaned, all depended.

My mind went back twenty years, to the day I first saw Griffith, who was then editing the *United Irishman*, and who had just printed my first attempt at journalism. The *United Irishman* is almost forgotten now, but it did its work. It was the beginning of everything and of everybody; it was the foundation of everything which in the next twenty years came to mean anything in Ireland. It was a paper of which every line was read, and was readable, of every week, and not perfunctorily, but with delight and avidity, a paper behind which was the impress of a master mind, plainly perceptible. It was the great trap set by the Irish national instinct to catch the young, and it did catch us. I remember a joke which Griffith got hold of about that time, which made everybody roar, but which had a profound truth behind it. He got hold of some circular or other of some Castle political department, in which people were warned in general terms to avoid too much conversation with "the man in the street." He printed it. I don't remember the exact wording of it now, but I do remember the exact wording of his *N.B.* to it. This was it: "N.B.—The street more particularly referred to is Fownes Street." 17 Fownes Street was the office of the *United Irishman*.

It was there that I first saw him, and there that I perceived the greatness of the man. It was a very small office on one of the upper floors, with an even smaller ante-room. There was just room enough for a desk and a couple of chairs—one window, very dusty; walls very dusty; dust everywhere. But the visitor never saw those things at first. Sitting at that desk, on a chair which mostly was rickety, was a small man, modest in appearance and in demeanour, unobtrusive, not remarkable until he looked full at you, and then you forgot everything save that powerful head, those hard, steadfast, balancing eyes. Here was power, intellect, and determination, and above all and behind all a sturdy commonsense, a commonness in the sense that you felt at once that here was that rare thing, a man of the people, bone of their bone, and flesh of their flesh, understanding them with all their national instinct and national sureness, their decency, and their absence of side, and yet the most powerful and steadfast intellect in Ireland. Here was a man who was all brain, and all good. The desk, the floor, the window recess, the mantel-piece, all full of files of papers—even the visitor's chair had to be apologetically cleared; against the wall at his left hand, bound files of his own paper, and in the middle of all this print and dust and quiet, this one man. I don't think that impression has ever left my mind, and I don't think it will ever leave the mind of any one of those who saw him as I did. The room looked to be in hopeless confusion, but that was only the appearance of it; he knew where everything was, and could lay his hands on anything when he wanted it.

At that time, the number of people who were consciously working for separation was very small. The Gaelic League, itself the most separatist organisation that ever existed in Ireland, and seen as such only by Griffith and his friends, was scornful of the "Tinpikemen," (Those who led the Gaelic League majority against us in those days are now violent Irregulars). There was a handful in Dublin, smaller groups in some country centres, and a fairly large group in London. Griffith, in the *United Irishman,* gave them cohesion, and direction, and enthusiasm; gave them true national education; was himself the foundation and the force of everything. Without him there would have been no movement.

The present generation knows not Griffith, and probably never will know him, though without him it would have been nothing. He was unemotional and unrhetorical, and he never in his life made a rhetorical appeal or an emotional appeal. He did not go about waving Republican flags and cursing England; but when, in his quiet, even, and decisive voice he said, "Let England take her right hand from Ireland's throat and her left hand out of Ireland's pocket," it was more effective and more understandable than any sword speech. And his pen was the most constructively-destructive pen that startled Ireland since Mitchel. Griffith has, in recent years, been spoken of as all sorts of things. He was really one thing—he was the Great Separatist, the most utterly separatist intellect that Ireland produced since Mitchel, who never wrote a line on any subject that was not a separatist line, and who never lost his grip upon reality. He was in his generation the supreme embodiment of his people.

Griffith supported Parnell. He supported Parnell because Parnell used the methods and means of his day—methods and means which were not essentially separatist—as a separatist and for separatist purposes; because Parnell, with his material and with his circumstances, advanced the separatist cause. He recognised that Parnell used the methods and materials of his time as a separatist would use them, and he held it to be good separatist policy to do that. So it is. The separatist is not necessarily he who shouts and blows up, but he who constructs, who uses. And Parnell, despite his oath of allegiance, was a separatist, because all his leading and all his intellect and all his achievement were separatist.

Griffith took the material of his own day, too—and its methods—and he fashioned them into the most comprehensive and constructive separatist philosophy that any subject nation has evolved. And he persisted. And he won. He forced England to "take her right hand from Ireland's throat and her left hand out of Ireland's pocket." He separated Ireland from England. He set out to do it, and persisted in it even when he could count his followers on his fingers and toes. He knew that Ireland would need him and need his policy. And when she needed him and it they were there. And in her service he spent himself.

In that final speech of his recommending the Treaty to Dáil Eireann, Griffith referred to Thomas Davis as his master; and while it may be said of all Irish nationalists that they are influenced by Davis, it was particularly true of Griffith, inasmuch as he believed passionately, with Davis, in not alone the desirability but the practicability of a union of all Irishmen against the domination of England. He was convinced of the innate patriotism of the Protestant and Unionist class in Ireland, and was convinced that a way could be found to unite them with the Nationalists upon the broad issue. And he was steeped in the philosophy of Davis and in the teaching of Davis. In himself he was an example of that teaching, for he knew Ireland, her capacity and resources, her history, her literature, her possibilities, as Davis recommends that all Irishmen should know her; and he gave his days and his nights to Ireland with a singlemindedness and a persistence which only a conviction that was a passion could have sustained.

The tragedy of the death of Arthur Griffith is not the tragedy of work unfinished, not the tragedy of a failure. He was always concerned with getting things done rather than with any particular concrete way of doing them, and in his efforts for Ireland he was concerned rather with achieving for Ireland freedom, than with achieving the triumph of any particular political formula or structure. When he said that "England must take one hand from off Ireland's throat and the other from out her pocket," he said exactly, and in its exact proportions, what he was aiming at; and at any time of his life he would have regarded any solution which gained that as an acceptable one. What he wanted was freedom for Ireland to develop on her own lines, free from outside interference; and it was that freedom, and not any particular way of embodying it, that he was concerned with.

He was one of the few Nationalists, for instance, who had any realization of the comparative value of economic freedom; and one of the things which he most consistently preached was that Ireland, by working unitedly on economic lines, could so develop her strength as to make it impossible for England to hold her. The tragedy of his death was not the tragedy of a failure, for he had succeeded in his object and in his policy: he had brought to Ireland a Treaty with England which made Ireland absolute mistress in her own house, with full economic and cultural freedom, and with practically full political freedom, and which, while it had to bow to circumstances in the matter of the Six Counties of Unionist Ulster, carried in itself the certainty of an eventual union of all Ireland. The tragedy in his death was this: that he who had loved Ireland so well and so passionately, who had been poor all his life for her sake, who had in the end raised her up, should have been struck down ere he enjoyed the glory of seeing her develop, of seeing all the things he loved to plan for her grow under his protecting hand. It is a lesser tragedy than that of any other Irish national leader.

Griffith has been written of as a non-believer in physical force. That is not true. He was a physical force man, and when I first knew him he was a member of the I.R.B., which he afterwards left, not on any point about physical force, but because after he had launched the Sinn Féin policy and established the Sinn Féin organisation he found the I.R.B. rule—that the Supreme Council has the right to dictate a policy to the members of the Brotherhood in public organisations—irksome. He was all his life a separatist and a physical force man of the old philosophic school, which held that physical force was permissible and necessary, that Ireland would eventually gain her independence only by means of it, but which

held also that a Rising by a minority was unjustifiable, save as
a demonstration, a blood-sacrifice—which the Rising of 1916
actually was. And the I.R.B never quarrelled with Griffith,
but always worked with him and recognised him for what he
was, the greatest separatist force in the country. As a matter
of fact, *Nationality*, which was established during the war and
edited by Griffith, was financed by the I.R.B.

It was a misfortune for Ireland that, when Sinn Féin was
reconstructed in 1917, the direction of it was taken out of
Griffith's hands. It could not have been done had he chosen
to fight against it. But he had Davis's passion for unity, provided what he regarded as essentials were preserved, and he
stood down rather than have even the semblance of a split,
though his credit and his reputation in the country were always
far greater than his modesty and diffidence would allow him
to realise; he could have carried Sinn Féin, on anything vital,
at any time against anybody. But, with the best intentions,
he stood down, and the direction of the movement fell into
the hands of men who had no philosophical nor trained nor
thought-out conception of nationalism, of means or of ends,
and who applied to every possible candidate for Dáil two tests:
(1) Was he ever in jail, or was he in the Rising, or was he in
the Volunteers? (2) Was he likely to be independent minded?
And if the answer to the first was "No" or to the second "Yes,"
he was barred. So that the Dáil came to be manned almost
wholly by people who, when their great test came, proved to
have neither moral courage nor political intelligence.

And that loss, the loss in the supreme direction of affairs of
his trained and Davisized mind, which had so fatal an effect
on Dáil, is the loss which Ireland felt most keenly. For Griffith
was the only member of the Government (save Eoin MacNeill,
who is too full of philosophical inertia to apply his national
philosophy) who had any philosophy of nationalism to rely
upon, who was in touch with the whole stream of Irish nationalist philosophy. In that respect he might be likened to a
grown up man amongst children.

Ave! Griffith. Ave atque Vale!

CHAPTER XXVI.

MICHAEL COLLINS.

When Mr. Edward Shortt projected his German Plot, Mick Collins was a man unknown save to a few. The Sinn Féin Executive of that day—it was before Dáil Eireann—knew that it was going to be arrested, and decided to stand on its dignity and be arrested, after naming substitutes. One man who was not on the Executive but was on the list of "plotters" decided not to be arrested. He waited in town until well on in the morning and then cycled home, to find a lorry standing outside his lodgings. From a halldoor on the opposite side of the street he watched them and then rode off to alarm another suspect, who, however, had been taken before he got there, and under whose roof the cyclist passed the remainder of the morning. It was Mick Collins. And it was the beginning of his emergence out of the ruck into that prominence which afterwards was his. The disappearance of the Sinn Féin Executive left in Sinn Féin and Volunteer circles one man in whose capable hands all the threads of the movement gradually became centred—as these things naturally will come to those who are capable and willing—and gradually but certainly Mick came to be the force and directing intelligence of the movement. And when the big guns were released finally, it made no difference. They had to admit Mick, for they could do nothing without him. He had made good. That is almost forgotten now, but to Mick Collins Ireland owed it that the movement went on when Mr. Shortt's German Plot made a clean sweep of its leaders. He worked, then and always, like three men, late and early, and he made others work also.

But it was in the succeeding years, the years of the Terror, that he finally found himself, that he did for Ireland that herculean labour which places him among her greatest. When Arthur Griffith stated in Dáil in January, 1922, that Collins had won the war, there was violent dissent. But, if any member of the Government or of the army or of Dáil can be said to have "won the war" it was Collins. His was the brain that conceived the war policy, and his the courage and determination and capacity that maintained it, and that never faltered in it. When it was projected, the Volunteer Executive would not sanction it, and Dáil Eireann would not touch it; but Mick Collins, and Dick McKee, and Seán Treacy organised it themselves, and put it into operation. And when it succeeded, then the wiseacres adopted it. But right through it Mick Collins was its eyes and its ears, its push and its determination, its support, its corner-stone. Everybody looked to him; everybody depended upon him. He represented to the people and to the British the embodied spirit of militant Irish nationalism, and he was that. It was not for nothing that the British got him on the brain, that they offered reward after reward for him, that in every house that they broke into they shouted, "Where's Mick Collins? We know he sleeps here." They were constantly hot on his trail; several times they actually had him in their hands; but they never "got" him. If one wants to realise what he meant to the movement then, one has only to look back and think what one would have felt like if they had got him. The whole bottom would have gone out of things. When de Valera was got just before the Truce, we said to each other, "Well, thank God it wasn't Mick."

Before Michael Coffins there lay an unknown future. He had other things besides his courage, his quickness of decision, his push, his character. He had a passion for efficiency which is rare in Ireland, and he had the rare power of attracting to him able men of all sorts who worked with and for him— often men who did not see eye to eye with him politically. His Department of Dáil Eireann was noted as the only one which, during the Terror, ever answered letters; so much so, that the country people wrote to him about everything—and he always saw to it that they were attended to. He gave as much attention to little details as most men do to the big things. And he was feeling his way towards a statesman's vision of Ireland. His record as organiser, as man of action, was a brilliant one, and his power of handling and vitalizing mediocrities was akin to that of Parnell.

But he was going farther than that. He was going from that to general speculation about Irish life, Irish character, Irish civilisation—he was feeling his way to a framing of that ideal of Ireland which in the coming years he would be working towards. He might have developed into the greatest and wisest statesman we ever had, for he was broadbased upon his love of the common people, the Irish peasantry, from whom he sprang, the people amongst whom he was brought up. On one of the last occasions on which I saw him, he tried to explain that; and obviously he found it difficult to put it in words. "I stand," said he (as nearly as I can recollect) " for an Irish civilisation based on the people and embodying and maintaining the things, their habits, ways of thought, customs, that make them different—the sort of life I was brought up in. That is what I mean by Irish Ireland, and if Irish Ireland means anything else, I don't want it. Once, years ago, a crowd of us were going along the Shepherd's Bush Road when out of a lane came a chap with a donkey—just the sort of donkey and just the sort of cart that they have at home. He came out quite suddenly and abruptly, and we all stood and cheered him. Nobody who has not been an exile will understand me, but I stand for that." There were in his brain and in his energy and in the whole Irishness of him—for Mick Collins was one of the most Irish men that ever lived—unexplored possibilities, incalculable riches.

But all that is dust now, and we have to remember him on his achievement. Let us remember him as the greatest soldier, the greatest man of action of the time of the Terror; the sure prop and resource of this nation in the time of the Terror; the man whose courage, resource, tireless energy, superhuman work, and push, enabled Ireland to outlast the British; and the man who, from the beginning to the end of this business, never said a bitter word.

CHAPTER XXVII.

THE VICTORY OF THE PEOPLE.

The question which was at issue in the civil war was not any question of Free State or Republic, but the question whether any ordered or settled Irish Government was possible; and it was the people's perception of that which rallied them to the Government and made the final and crushing defeat of the Irregulars possible—and not alone possible, but inevitable. We had used Irregular methods ourselves with the support of the people, in 1920 and 1921, for the purpose of destroying a foreign Government, a Government which had no moral nor constitutional sanction, depending solely upon force; and if it proved to be possible for a minority of ourselves successfully to use these methods against a constitutional Government democratically selected, there was an end to any possibility of stable government here. The victory of the people was a victory for democratic government as against a military despotism, a victory for the ballot as against the bullet.

In gaining that victory, in the circumstances, the people gave evidence of possessing character and judgment. During the whole of the war—and before it and after it for that matter—the Irregular propagandists had practically a free field. Government propaganda was both inadequate and unintelligent, and the Irregulars were allowed to annex, without dispute, every nationalist principle and phrase which had been the common property of the separatist movement for generations. The people who were striking at the very life of the nation were allowed to pose as the pure-souled patriots; while those who upheld the nation did so in a sort of sackcloth-and-ashes.

So that the people's support of the Government was a support which was not materially Government-aided, but arose out of the people's own perception of the situation.

To the Government itself, the untried and unknown group who carried the burthen after the deaths of Griffith and Collins, Ireland owes more than she will ever understand in our time. In the lifetime of the two leaders, the others had neither power nor responsibility. Suddenly, in the middle of a civil war, they had to take over one of the most difficult situations that ever confronted any Government, knowing that upon them depended whether the nation was to live or to perish ignobly in a savage welter of blood. And they rose to their responsibilities and carried the thing through to a finish, taking, without complaint, the responsibility for the unpopular things they had to do in order to save the nation. As a Government they have never had fair play (no Irish Government for thirty or forty years will get that), and have had to carry on, not alone against Irregular propaganda, but against general and mostly unfair criticism from their own friends. And that continues in the peace. We do not seem to have yet developed any civic sense, any general realisation of the responsibilities of Government, so that what passes for criticism is only opposition on principle, opposition to everything whether it is right or wrong. We have been so long criticising Governments with the knowledge that whatever we said we could neither affect them nor impair their credit, that we fail to realise that an Irish Government has a right to more intelligent treatment from its own people, and that the sort of criticism we are giving it impairs not alone the Government's efficiency but the credit of the nation.

Of the things which the Government did in the civil war, nothing has been more sharply and unfairly criticised than the executions. The Irregulars themselves assumed that because they posed as pure-souled patriots they were at liberty to commit every crime in the calendar, while their opponents were bound to turn the other cheek and behave like Christians; and the criticism of the executions accepts, consciously or unconsciously, that claim. Now, it may be argued that the executions were unwise, but it certainly cannot be argued that they were illegal. They were carried out with the authority of the Dáil, by virtue of a Resolution passed by Dáil, and clearly explained to and understood by Dáil before it passed it, and there is therefore no question of their legality. Whether the execution of young country lads, members of the rank-and-file of the Irregulars, served any really useful purpose is a question much more open to doubt. But the critics usually say very little about that; what they fasten on being the reprisal execution of Rory O'Connor, Mellowes, Barrett, and MacKelvey. Now, that reprisal execution seems to me to have been illegal, but there is no doubt whatever that it was right and just: because these four were amongst the leaders who were responsible for the split and the attempt to set up a minority tyranny, O'Connor and Mellowes in particular having a responsibility for the whole development of the split inferior only to that of De Valera and Brugha. O'Connor, Mellowes, and Brugha were tampering with the army before even the final vote had been taken in the Dáil on the Treaty.

If somebody had to suffer, it was just that the leaders should suffer. The men who deserved execution were the paper warriors, the men who issued the instructions which the rank-and-file carried out, and the men who, being civil leaders, supported and approved of those instructions, some of whom are yet informing the country that they will do a hundred million pounds' worth of damage the *next time,* instead of fifty millions' worth. It was wrong—though it was legal—to execute young boys for obeying the orders of those whom they acknowledged as their leaders while many of these same leaders, captured after the Act became law, and morally and actually responsible for the bloodshed and the savagery, were spared.

Those who criticised the Government's execution policy were, for the most part, humbugs. They were the people who had been criticising them for months before there were any executions, for not having an execution policy. And whatever genuine criticism there was, forgot altogether one thing: that this war against the Irish people was an insurrection against the sovereignty of the people and against a Government which, on the point at issue, represented the overwhelming mass of the people. By ordinary law and ordinary precedent, the lives of everybody taking part in that insurrection were forfeit, and in any ordinary country the Irregulars would have been shot down summarily as they were taken, without the formality of a trial. That the majority of them are still alive they owe to the fact that the first Irish Government was a Government which, in the face of great provocation, displayed extraordinary clemency and moderation.

The victory of the Irish Government over the Irregulars was the victory of the ballot over the bullet, and the establishment of democratic machinery of government as against Donnybrook Fair. It was not a victory for the Treaty any more than it was a defeat for the Republic, because neither of these was at stake. It was a victory for the decision by the people, through the ordinary democratic machinery of the day, of their own affairs.

CHAPTER XXVIII.

THE HUMOROUS SIDE.

The whole thing—the post-truce bellicosity, the new "I.R.A.," the Great Talk, and the Irregulars—had a humorous side which should not go quite unchronicled. I have referred already to the way in which many people who, during the "Tan" war, were "civil and strange" with Sinn Féin, and who had wavered between the Extreme Right and the Centre, after the Truce went over to the Extreme Left, and began to feel like heroes. Then there were the men who had been in Sinn Féin at some time or another, and who had fallen out when it looked dangerous, or who had some sort of questionable political past. And there were the men who had not fought in 1916, and who could not afford to follow their convictions a second time. Then there were the artist-poets and the poet-artists and all that Art class who had always looked down upon "politics" and had hitherto had no connection with it—save to write a sonnet when everything was over. They, who had remained stiffly and superiorly outside Sinn Féin while the British remained in Ireland—who had done nothing whatever to help—now asked each other, "Was it for this *we* fought?" and talked mournfully about "betrayal." And then there were the aliens—the English, French, and American wives of Irish citizens, mostly without any history as Irishwomen—who paid their tribute to the charm of Irish civilization by being *Hibernicis ipsis hiberniores,* and calling upon the world to witness that *they,* at least, would never accept this dishonourable compromise. "Surely we are not going to accept this. Was it for this . . . ?" etc.

It is perhaps characteristic of the women pseudo-Republicans that their great contribution to laughter was a thing upon which they prided themselves as an especially heroic and meritorious proceeding. They contributed the cut direct. The pseudo-Republican man never quite lost his sociability. He was always willing to make a truce and argue, or even eat, with you. He knew that he was not exactly the salt of the earth and did not pretend to be. But when the pseudo-Republican woman saw you coming, up went her nose in the air and she passed you by, pluming herself on her self-sacrifice in breaking another friendship "for the cause," when all the time she was only demonstrating that her consciousness of her own hypocrisy was so ever-present that she could not bear to look in the face somebody who had had the moral courage not to be a hypocrite. The man, as the woman, who is afraid to meet the eye of a political opponent, has a guilty conscience.

CHAPTER XXIX.

THE RESPONSIBILITY OF MR. DE VALERA.

Thy hand, great Anarch, lets the curtain fall
And universal darkness buries all.

A country may forget, and forget quickly, the most appalling of physical calamities. Earthquake, pestilence, famine, foreign oppression, military defeat, anything traceable to the hand of God or the hand of man is as if it had not been once it has passed away; but there is one exception to that, and that is civil war. Civil war tears and lacerates and tortures for generations. It is something so unspeakably vile that no theology can envisage it as from the hand of God. It comes from the devilish heart of man, from pride and stubbornness and egoism and selfishness. Lucifer made the first civil war, and Luciferian are all civil wars.

Many things contributed to the civil war in Ireland. For one thing, Sinn Féin succeeded too quickly and too easily, and it was not prepared for that. The bulk of the Sinn Féiners in 1921, were people with no nationalist history worth speaking about, with no nationalist tradition, and with no conception of the amount of hard and unpaid work that had gone to the laying of the foundations. They saw only the success and the guns and the glory. The small handful of leaders who had directed the movement were not prepared for success. They were ready to die, were ready to go out into the wilderness and remain out in the wilderness upholding the separatist banner, and would have been content to do that had they not had so overwhelming a success—had England persevered and broken the Volunteers—but they had never planned nor prepared for a taking over of an Irish Constitution which should be less than separation and yet only a little less. That there should be

differences of opinion in Sinn Féin when confronted with the
Treaty was inevitable; but that these differences should be
decided by civil war was not alone not inevitable but was
unnatural. The responsibility for that civil war lies almost
altogether on Eamon de Valera.

When the Treaty was signed, there lay upon Mr. de Valera
one of the heaviest responsibilities ever laid upon any Irish
leader. Since 1917 the titular leadership of Ireland had been
bestowed on him. He was not the real leader. The real leaders
were Griffith and Collins, who had carried the nation through
the "Tan" war while de Valera was in America; and especially
Collins, who was the brain and the inspiration of the whole
business. But Collins was primarily a man of action, blunt
and outspoken, and Griffith was equally blunt. Mr. de Valera
was the Bayard, the trumpet, the maker of beautiful phrases,
the enunciator of principles, the Irish Wilson. His power, for
good or evil was immense, and it was founded, as Wilson's was,
on his appeal to high moral principles—on his spellbinding.

Mr. de Valera never had much illusion as to Sinn Féin's
chance of winning. He knew, when the Great War ended,
that the best hope then lay in pinning Wilson to his principles
at Versailles. He knew, when Wilson wriggled out, that the best
chance then was to appeal to America to put into force in
Ireland those Wilsonian principles which had brought America
into the war. He knew, when America turned us down, that
there was no further hope of complete victory. He had always
had, in his own mind, the idea that it might be necessary for
Ireland to accept less than independence, and for a minority
of Sinn Féin to go out into the wilderness and maintain the
movement for separation. He had been the first publicly to
suggest to England that she should offer Ireland less than
independence; had said privately, before the Truce, that he
would not be the man to oppose a Dominion; had sent Harry
Boland back to America during the negotiations with
instructions to prepare American opinion for a settlement
which would not be complete independence. When Mr. Lloyd
George's first letter to him came, he knew that it meant settlement. He knew when he went over to see Mr. Lloyd George,

that he would not be discussing independence with him, and he knew when he came back, just how far Mr. Lloyd George was likely to go. He knew; when the Plenipotentiaries went over, that they could not bring back independence, and he opposed every attempt in Dáil to bind them to independence or to limit their powers. But in the final hour he changed. He stabbed in the back the men he had sent over to do what they had done, knowing well what was the most they could accomplish, knowing well that they had accomplished more than he or anybody else had deemed possible when he sent them over, knowing well that although the actual signatures to that Treaty were those of Griffith and Collins the real signature was that of de Valera—that the Treaty was in reality *his* creation more than that of any other Irishman. In the annals of political treachery there is no parallel to that.

He was moved, I think, by a variety of reasons. As far back as 1917 or 1918 he had believed, and he had expressed his belief, that it would be necessary eventually for "some of us to go back into the wilderness" while the main body of the nation worked some scheme which was less than independence. That idea probably remained in his subconsciousness. But in 1921 he was not the unsophisticated Bayard he had been before he went America. He had gained in polish, in rhetoric, in platform tricks, in vanity and egoism—but he had lost in simplicity and honesty. He had succumbed somewhat to that vice of degeneration to which every politician is subject There is no doubt that up to the latest stage of the negotiations he was for settlement—even so late as a couple of days before the Treaty was signed he was asking Bishops whether he would be right in holding out on customs and excise—there is equally no doubt that after the departure of Collins and Griffith he was exposed to a great deal of post-Truce bellicosity. In the light of that bellicosity, things that were obviously impossible in July, 1921, things which Brugha and Stack and Mary MacSwiney, no less than de Valera and Griffith and Collins, had agreed were not within reach, seemed in December to have been within reach. What Mr. de Valera himself said at the time with regard to his own process of thought may not inopportunely find its place here.

For some time before the Treaty was signed, Mr. P. J. Little, editor of *New Ireland*, had been in South Africa on a Dáil mission. He had asked me to write the weekly "Notes" pages for the paper in his absence, and I had been doing so. When the Treaty was signed, I wrote for *New Ireland* the "comments" (which I reprint in the Appendix to this book), and a couple of weeks later Mr. Little returned. He asked me to go on writing the notes for the time being, until he got a grip of the situation. I agreed, but said: "You know the sort of notes I have been writing?" " Yes," said he, "go ahead for the present." I went ahead for a couple of weeks more, and then I met Mr. Little in the street. He told me that he was still unable to make up his mind, and he also told me Mr. de Valera's explanation to him. According to Mr. Little, Mr. De Valera told him that in all his negotiations with Mr. Lloyd George, he had been playing a Machiavelian game, that he had never intended to accept anything less than a Republic, and that what he had been aiming at was to screw the highest possible offer out of Lloyd George and then to drop him. I asked Mr. Little whether he believed that, and he said he did not know; but a week later he did make up his mind, and he joined the pseudo-Republicans. That, at any rate, was Mr. de Valera's defence at the time to Mr. Little. I have no doubt that he made different defences to different people. But that particular one, at any rate, is rescued. It is, obviously, not true.

I was at the Dáil when the final vote was taken, and I watched Mr. de Valera. His demeanour was that of a man taken completely by surprise, and wounded in his tenderest part—his vanity. I could see no trace of anything noble or fundamental in him, but only the petulance of wounded vanity. It was unbelievable, to him, and not to be borne, that he should be beaten in a straight vote in Dáil. It was unbelievable to him, also, that there should be in Ireland a Government without himself as President of it. He was ready to do anything to prevent that, and he went to all lengths to prevent it.

He had known all along that in the end there would have to be a settlement which was less than independence. He had welcomed the Lloyd George letter because it led to that, and

he had told Dáil as plainly as that could be done in an
indirect way, that he was going to compromise. He meant to
compromise. But he himself pandered to the gallery. He
spoke, and he wrote, things which he never meant, things
which were only in order to solidify public opinion and induce
England to come a bit farther, and he raised up an irresponsible Left which, when the time came, he had not the
moral courage to put in its place. What might have been only
a difference of opinion he made into a disastrous split. If every
effort had been made privately to come to some common
agreement on the Treaty, there never need have been a split;
but Mr. de Valera wanted a split, and he insisted upon publicity.
His first pronouncement, the recall of the delegates, asked for
a split. People who, that morning, were satisfied with the
Treaty, were delighted with it, recognising it as an astonishing
achievement in the circumstances, changed completely in the
afternoon when Mr. de Valera's bombshell appeared in the
evening papers. *It* pointed to a split. Mr. de Valera's further
publicity made the split, and every proceeding of his worsened
it. At a time when no responsible person thought of such a
thing as civil war, Mr. de Valera was at pains to remind us that
we had now a "constitutional way of settling our differences."
That was only an oblique reminder of the fact that there was
another way, and its effect was instantly to turn the irresponsibles amongst the pseudo-Republicans to the other way.

In the months between the ratification of the Treaty and the
outbreak of the civil war, Mr. de Valera went from bad to
worse. Knowing that the country was against him, he tried to
muzzle it. He would agree neither to a plebiscite nor to an
election, and he deliberately created conditions which made
either impossible. He threw overboard democracy and declared
for minority rule, and he formed an army which was avowedly
a terrorising army, an army which avowedly meant to force the
Irish people to do a thing which they did not wish to do. He
used every trick and every threat to delay an election, and to
hamper the Provisional Government in its functioning.

For the civil war, the whole responsibility is on Mr. de
Valera. Its proximate cause may have been Thompson's

Garage, or it may have been anything else, but its real cause was Mr. de Valera's refusal to accept majority decision, his appeal to violence, his rejection of democratic procedure, his formation of a Terrorist army, and his failure to control that army. He was the moral force and the voice behind the whole pseudo-Republican-Irregular movement.

CHAPTER XXX.

THE IRISH FREE STATE.

At the end of May, 1923, the Irregulars collapsed, beaten out of the field, in a cloud of blasphemy to which the names of Mr. de Valera and Mr. Frank Aikin were appended; and at the General Election in August of that year, at which the issue was the Treaty and the Constitution, they secured less than one-third of the seats. The judgment of Dáil in ratifying the Treaty against Mr. de Valera's advice was thus vindicated, and the Irish Free State was established by a free vote of the people. That it was established at all, in the circumstances, is a tremendous tribute to the fundamental good sense of the people, and to the patriotism and determination of that Provisional Cabinet which carried on, against Cain, the struggle for national existence after the death of Griffith and Collins, and which flinched neither from the unpopularity which the hard things they had to do brought them at the time nor from the ingratitude which they knew would be their portion from those whom they had saved once the danger was past.

For the first time since the landing of Strongbow there is in Ireland a National Authority and a National Constitution menaced by no external power, and safeguarded by Treaty against the one power which menaced Ireland since Strongbow; and for the first time since the Patriot Parliament of 1689, there exists in Ireland a Parliament which is not only Irish and free, but is also representative and is responsible to the people of Ireland and to none but the people of Ireland. Between the Constitution of the Irish Free State and the problematical one of an Irish Republic the difference is so microscopic that, for practical purposes, it does not exist; and the powers of government which the Oireachtas now possesses in Ireland would not be extended by the achievement of complete independence. Its power over finance, over education, over Irish affairs generally, is complete and absolute, and independent of any external power or influence. However much the pseudo-Republicans may dislike it, we are now a free people; and despite all their fustian and braggadocio and terrorism, the Irish Free State and its Constitution are firmly established, and remain the only instruments through which the further advance to complete independence may be made.

The limitations placed upon Ireland's full freedom by the Treaty are more verbal than actual. The much discussed oath is an oath of allegiance to the Irish Constitution, and one of fidelity to the British King, not in his capacity as King of Great Britain, but in his capacity as head of the British Commonwealth of Nations. It is nothing but eyewash. It was devised to save faces, to save Lloyd George's face by enabling him to say: But those fellows are accepting the King; and to save Mr. de Valera's face by enabling him as if to say:—We are giving neither allegiance nor fidelity to the King of England. We are giving fidelity to the head of the British Commonwealth of Nations, so long as we chose to remain in that Commonwealth. Our allegiance is to the Irish Constitution, and that alone. This is the sort of oath which the independent kings of the smaller European states in the middle ages used to take to the Holy Roman Emperor.—The other things are formalities which have to be maintained so long as we are not completely independent, but which do not affect our powers under the Constitution. The people who have made such a noise about them have neither honesty nor a sense of humour. Take, for instance, all the fuss about the Governor-General and his establishment. Such as he is, the Governor-General is neither a Governor nor a General. He is a legal fiction, a sort of rubber stamp, who is as absolutely the slave of the Executive Council as if he were really a rubber stamp. And that the people who sent fifty million pounds up in smoke, and declare that they will send a hundred millions next time, and regard themselves as first-class heroes, should make the welkin ring at the thought of paying ten thousand a year to "Tim" Healy, is one of the most Gilbertian items in a situation which was, and is, full of tragical humour.

The oath itself is one of the most harmless oaths ever devised. The pseudo-Republicans fastened upon it for the sake of propaganda, and elevated it into an anti-English test—not because they really cared a damn about it, but because they thought that it would win them support. It was they, and their lying propaganda that moved England to insist on the oath, as she was entitled to do under the strict letter of the Treaty; and it is they and their hypocrisy and their lying that is responsible for the fact that the Irish Government, in its handling of foreign affairs, has found itself unable to act as vigorously as it should, and as it would like to. A government which is fighting for its life against internal treachery cannot give any attention to external policy; and at a time when it was vital that the Irish Government should have the support of every Irish citizen, at a time when the details were being framed of a Constitution which was to govern Ireland, and which the pseudo-Republican leaders knew would govern Ireland for some time to come, they were concentrated on the congenial task of stabbing in the back the first Irish Government. The pseudo-Republicans did not want a good Constitution, because they calculated that a bad one would gain them support, and so they worked against a good Constitution; they did not want a united Ireland, because they calculated that Partition would give them support, and so they worked against any conciliation with the Six Counties; they did not want normal settled conditions, because they calculated that distress and discontent would gain them support, and so they fomented strikes and civil commotion and unrest of all sorts. Danton, in a memorable moment, said in the Revolutionary Chamber: "Let us die, if necessary, so that the country be free." What our sea-green incorruptible hypocrites said, was: "Let the country die, if necessary, so that we get our own way."

But the Provisional Government, and the Irish Free State, survived their assaults and their treacheries. And the Irish

Free State stands as the most tremendous achievement of any generation of Irishmen. It is Ireland with England's one hand off her throat and the other hand out of her pocket. It is Ireland, at long last, free and unhampered in the management of her own affairs and in the development of her own resources.

CHAPTER XXXI.

HOW IT STRIKES A CONTEMPORARY.

The preceding chapters of this book are, I am afraid, somewhat disjointed. That arises partly from the complexity of the subject—difficult to deal with concisely and lucidly—and partly from the fact that the book has been written at short intervals, in spurts, under great difficulties. In this chapter I am going to record how the whole business strikes me, and if in doing so I restate things already stated, I think they will gain from being all put together; and I think that the book would be incomplete (it would, at any rate, not be the book I planned) without this chapter—repetitions and all.

I had better say, first, why I regard myself as a contemporary whose opinion it is worth while setting down—why I think that that opinion will be of interest to that unborn generation to whom this book is dedicated. I belong to that small minority of people who founded the modern separatist movement, and fostered it, and educated it, and slaved for it, and beggared themselves for it. I was a member of the National Council which Griffith formed in 1902, and which was the practical beginning of Sinn Féin organisation. I was a member of the Executives of Cumann na nGaedheal (the separatist organisation which grew out of the Celtic Literary Societies), of the Dungannon Clubs (the separatist Sinn Féin organisation of 1906), and of the Sinn Féin League (the organisation which was formed by the union of Cumann na nGaedheal and the Dungannon Clubs). I was a member of the Executive of Sinn Féin, the organisation which was formed by the union of the Sinn Féin League and the National Council. I was a member of the Supreme Council of the I.R.B. from 1908 until my deportation in 1914. I wrote in all Griffith's papers (the *United Irishman, Sinn Féin,* and *Nationality*); wrote extensively in W. P. Ryan's *The Peasant* and *Nation*; edited, with Pat McCartan and Bulmer Hobson, *Irish Freedom* 1911 to 1914); edited *An Saoghal Gaedhealach* (1918–1919) and *The Separatist* (1922). I was one of the small band of civil servants (they could be counted on the fingers of one man) who resigned the service in 1919 rather than take the British oath of allegiance. I worked in the Gaelic League and in the Gaelic Athletic Association equally with the political movement, and since 1902 have been intimately in touch with every phase of the general movement.

In these circumstances I am, I think, entitled to presume that a record of how it strikes me will be of sufficient interest to warrant me in setting it down. It will, at any rate, be a record from somebody who does know something about the movement, whose point of view is entirely friendly, whose record of work in the movement is second to that of no living man, but who is not prepared now, any more than at any previous time, to shirk the truth, however unpleasant it may be.

The Sinn Féin movement was essentially a constructive, educational, intellectual movement. Its philosophy was the philosophy of Thomas Davis. Its sustaining force was love for Ireland and desire to serve her. Its ideals were pure, and its workers were utterly unselfish and utterly unpaid. It had no hatreds. Although Griffith, and indeed all of us, wrote bitterly and scathingly about England and about the Irish Parliamentary Party, we had no hatred for either. We loved the Protestant as well as Catholic, nay better than, for Tone was the first of modern nationalists, and remains the chief; and Protestant names lie thick on the separatist roll of honour. The incredibly diabolical mental processes of the Irregular mind of the last two years would have been utterly alien to us.

It is easy for people who, until two or three years ago, were scornfully pro-British to talk now about "the Republic," and all the rest of the cant into which they have turned the principles they defile. They have no tradition and no philosophy and no experience. They have no conception of the hard work it all involved. They knew nothing of the movement until it had become the popular movement, until everybody supported it, even the Pulpit and the Press. I can remember it in other circumstances. I remember the heartbreaking effort, year after year, to keep the movement going, to keep its branches alive; I remember Griffith living on thirty shillings a week—and often not getting that—and his paper constantly on the point of death for want of as many pounds per year as these people dissipated in a single "stunt" or "job": I remember the apathy and the scorn everywhere, and the opposition. I remember when the number of people who did as much as an annual hand's turn for Irish independence did not go beyond three figures. I remember the ragged and underfed regiments— the men who died from overwork, and the men who, through poverty and overwork, managed to survive—to be elbowed out by the mob.

Enthusiasm, honesty, youth, and a coherent national policy, a policy which was capable of being adapted to meet any change of conditions, sustained us. Sinn Féin was founded on two things—on the Irish language and all the tradition and national individuality which that brings with it, and on the will to be free. We knew that no foreign government can govern a nation unless the people themselves help that government or suffer it; and we knew that our problem was to get a majority of our people to declare that they would do neither. We knew that a clear majority, using constructively the powers Ireland already possessed, and assuming to itself such other powers as Ireland could give it, would force England to give up her hold on Ireland. But we never really expected to see it in our time.

When the General Election of 1918 gave Sinn Féin a majority, it gave it under the most favourable conditions possible. It gave it enthusiasm, the fervour of new converts, wild popular support, and all the dash and impetus of a quick victory In three years a thing had happened which ought to have taken three generations. Sinn Féin had the power, it had the material, it had the will, and it had the policy; and yet it, while attaining the great success of the Treaty, missed that greater success which was in its grasp and achieved a disaster unparalleled. Why? The answer is, because it did not keep its physical force element in its proper place, but allowed it to dictate policy and to crowd out the civil side. Before 1916, we had too little physical force, and after 1916 we had far too much.

The place of physical force in separatist philosophy, prior to 1916, was a subordinate place. It was a line of action, but it was not the only nor the main line of action; it was, rather, a last reserve. Nobody pretended to believe that we could fight England physically, nobody pretended to believe that an insurrection would be anything but suicide for those taking part in it; but the philosophy of the blood sacrifice, which most people seem to think originated with Pearse, was an essential part of separatist philosophy. The use of arms, and the right to insurrect, were maintained as a matter of principle, but rather as a means of arousing the nation's soul than as a policy. I remember discussions on it at Supreme Council meetings long before 1916, when we were trying to shape things towards some definite goal. And it was agreed then that it was our duty to make a forlorn hope insurrection if the time came when some such desperate measures were necessary in order to recall the nation to self-respect and decency. That was the physical force philosophy prior to 1916, and it was sound.

1916 gave Ireland the forlorn hope insurrection which had been advocated; and, thanks to England's stupidity, it had the effect which the Supreme Council, in adopting the policy, had hoped it would have. It restored Ireland's self-respect and awakened her soul. It pledged the majority of her people to Sinn Féin and independence. It placed political power in the hands of people who could be trusted to use it in the furtherance of independence. Its work was done.

After 1916, there should not have been a shot fired in Ireland, nor a gun bought.[1] They were totally unnecessary. We

---

[1.] I should like to say that this is not being wise after the event. I was out of Ireland from 1914 to 1918, but in 1917, the first year I was allowed home, I made this statement to my brother (afterwards O.C. No.1 Cork Brigade), and in the winter of 1918 I made it to Mick Collins after becoming aware in conversation of the direction his plans were taking. Both of these, of course, scoffed at me.

had the Sinn Féin policy, the men who made it, the enthusiasm and the support of the people. Without firing a shot we could have forced from England anything that we have forced from her by the gun policy, and more. We would, at the same time, have maintained our solidarity, escaped Partition, and avoided the irreparable moral disaster which has overtaken us. But for the lack of a firm hand on the civil side of the movement, no effort to control the gun was made, and it brought us to disaster. The Dáil of 1919 was a national assembly with full authority from the people. Every national unit in the country was bound to obey it. It, and it alone, was entitled to give directions about policy. But the policy which brought disaster— the guerilla-war-ambush-and-shooting-of-civilians policy—was adopted without reference to Dáil, and was not controlled by Dáil, although Dáil had to accept responsibility for it, and although it was assumed by the public at large that Dáil had sanctioned the policy. The longer the war went on the worse it got and the more fatal its effects. By the winter of 1920 the popular games amongst the Dublin children were ambush games. The most popular of these was a game in which one player was supposed to be an old gentleman, and the others, armed with guns, held him up and declared, "Alan Bell, your time has come." There it was—the writing on the wall—staring us in the face and we did not see it. It marked the moral degradation of the young. And by the spring of 1921 our women were in that frame of mind I have written of in another chapter, thinking death, planning death, organising for wounds and blood and cruelty. That marked the moral degradation of the women. Those gave us the worst excesses of Irregularism, and they will trouble us for many a year to come.

Then when, in 1921, victory came, victory as overwhelming as it was unexpected, the position might have been retrieved had the gunman been told how near he had gone to ruining everything. Instead of which he was hailed as a saviour, told how he had won the war, and invited to multiply himself, and to spread himself into all the counties wherein he had been, in the actual war, nominal, So that when the Treaty was signed, there was a mass of post-Truce bellicosity spread over

the country, idle—to a large extent drunken—and easy
material for an explosion.

Mr. de Valera supplied the match. He did not mean to.
He was only trying to frighten people, to influence votes, to
manœuvre the Treaty people from using their popular majority.
The one aim the Anti-Treaty Party had was to prevent an
appeal to the people on the Treaty issue, because they knew
they would be hopelessly beaten on any such appeal; and in
attempting to compass this, Mr. de Valera threw all decency,
all caution, all honesty to the winds. He allowed his followers
to secede from the army, and to form a Terrorist army. He
allowed that Terrorist army to commit acts of Terrorism—to
"commandeer" buildings, food, and supplies; to attack members
of the National Army, to fulminate as if they had popular or
democratic support. It was easy for them to go further. They
knew no law but the gun, and they respected no civilian unless
he, too, could produce a gun. They robbed banks. They robbed
post offices. They robbed private houses and business houses.
They blew up "enemy" *(i.e.,* Irish citizens') residences, business
houses and vehicles. They blew up his picture houses. They
blew up his trains, his roads, his bridges. They declared him
an outlaw, to be shot at sight. They were, frankly, Frankenstein.

We ourselves, in our own blindness and folly, were responsible for that Frankenstein. We taught our young people to
rely on the gun and to disregard everything else! We set up
irresponsible and inexperienced and unbalanced youths as
"Brigadiers" and "O.C.'s" with power of life and death over
whole counties: we glorified ambushes and "stunts" and "jobs"
and secret executions without trial: we abolished all the
ordinary laws of morality, and of public decency, and of social
responsibility, without setting up anything in their place save
the exigencies of military policy interpreted by any irresponsible
Brigadier or O.C.: we created a situation wherein our civilisation was ripe, because of the weakening of the ordinary
established safeguards, for reversion to a primitive unorganised
society in which everything would depend upon force—a state
of society such as that pictured powerfully and prophetically
by H. G. Wells in the last chapter of his *War in the Air.* The

things which ordinarily hold civilisation together were gone, they had been undermined unconsciously, and it needed only somebody to pull out the final prop to set the whole structure tumbling.

That was Mr. de Valera's proud achievement. His was the brain which, in the first days of the Treaty, before there was even a split, reminded everybody that there was a way, other than by the ballot box, to settle any differences of opinion on the Treaty; his the brain, and his the voice, which encouraged and organised disorder and indiscipline, which prevented the issue from being decided in the ordinary democratic way; his the brain, and his the voice, which invited his followers to wade through the blood of their comrades and of the members of the Provisional Government. Ireland would not dance to his tune, and therefore would he send her to hell.

Ireland has always had plenty of physical courage. That has never been supplemented by moral courage. Since 1916 we have been damned by successive layers of irresponsible gunmen without ideas, and political leaders without moral courage. The men of 1916 were idealists, men who were in the movement from conviction and not as the result of an emotional wave, men who had consecrated their lives to Ireland from a sense of duty and patriotism. Their leaders would never have agreed to the beastly things that were done afterwards.[2] The men of 1918 to 1921 were different. They included, for the first time, the gunman and the irresponsible and the moral degenerate, people whose nationalism was founded neither in knowledge nor conviction, but in the parrot-cry of "Up the Republic!" They included a proportion of men who had not been out in 1916, and who *afterwards* wished they had, and felt that they had to be violent and extreme in order to make up for their failure—as they had come to regard it—in 1916. They looked down on the 1916 men as amateurs and bunglers. Then the

[2.] On the march to the G.P.O. in 1916, Sean MacDermott was asked to sanction the shooting of G-man Hoey, who was across the street. He refused, and swore at the man who proposed it. It was Hoey, ironically enough, who afterwards picked Sean out of a draft of prisoners who were departing for internment at Frongoch.

1922 men came along as a third layer. They were the people
who had not been out before that, who *now* wished they had,
and who were the product of the years of war and unrest and
moral loosening we had had. They looked down on all their
predecessors as babes, and when they themselves got going
they made them look like babes. We have been living under
what was practically a military Terrorism, in which a civilian
government existed merely as a machine for registering military decrees, and under which every argument save the gun
was eliminated.

Up to 1916, Sinn Féin was an unselfish and spiritual and
constructive movement. After 1916, it gradually changed. It
became a mob movement, run by a political machine more
effective and more unscrupulous, and more intolerant of ability
and independent judgment, than even the Parliamentarian
movement had been. That political machine, in its turn,
became a tool in the hands of the military side of the movement; so that, in the end, the whole thing was moulded by
men who were incapable of regarding democratic government
seriously only in so far as it could be manipulated, or forced,
to do what the military mind wanted.

On the other hand, our political leaders had no moral
courage, and no foresight. After England had won the war,
they must have known that we had no chance of achieving
independence and that, sooner or later, terms of some sort
would have to be made; but they made no attempt to prepare
their followers or the public for that, although conversations
began in the autumn of 1920 and were never broken off.
When the Truce came, and they knew that "the Republic" was
in the background for the present, they had not the courage
to say so unequivocally, and they had not the courage to throw
cold water on that wave of hysterical post-Truce bellicosity
which was to poison Mr. de Valera's mind, throw the women
into further hysteria, and end in disaster. When the Treaty
came eventually they had not the courage to face it and take
the responsibility which it involved. The one side, the more
culpable side, took on the pose of sea-green incorruptibles,
and while they promulgated a settlement which was worse

than the Treaty, talked and postured about that Republic which, in the dark days of July, 1921, they had recognised had to go overboard. The other side, while recognising that there was no rational alternative to the Treaty, while working for the Treaty, facing calumny and misrepresentation and death for the sake of the people, had not the courage to be honest about the Treaty. They, too, talked about the Republic, and about the Government of the Republic, and the army of the Republic—thus jeopardising their own position, bewildering the people, and playing into the hands of Mr. de Valera.

The end was disaster. It was a disaster of our own making. Pride, and ignorance, and selfishness, and shallowness, and gun worship—these made it. When the English invaded Ireland and had got started on their bloody career, a Synod of the Irish Church decided that the invasion was a punishment by God because of the Irish raiding the coasts of Britain for slaves. The visitation which we have gone through was the result of our own breaches of the Moral Law. There are certain things which should not be done, even to obtain freedom. We did them, and they seemed to succeed, and we went on doing them. *We have paid.* And we must get away—we are getting away—from all that worship of physical force, application of force, contempt for life, for decency, for charity and tolerance, which have made of our country a moral and physical slaughter-house.

We have slain Frankenstein, and buried him. We have shed all our illusions about "the Island of Saints" and "Rich and rare were the gems she wore." We know now that we are just like other people, that the beast in us is restrained only by the same sanctions and conventions which restrain him elsewhere. We have, for the first time, on us the responsibility and the reality of government. And the future is still ours.

CHAPTER XXXII.

THE FUTURE OF IRELAND.

The people of my own generation who will read this book, will expect this chapter to be a discourse on the political future or Ireland. Save in one particular, that of Partition, that seems to me to be now of comparatively small importance. What has mattered in political freedom has been the power to develop our own resources, shape our own destinies, and preserve our own distinctive nationality. And that power we now have, all verbiage to the contrary notwithstanding. But, at the same time, there need be no doubt in the mind of anybody what our future will be. Ireland is a nation, not of to-day or yesterday, but of the dawn, and her civilisation is old and virile and her traditions deep-rooted. She will not remain a permanent member of the British Commonwealth—nor of any similar group. She is intensely individualistic and aggressive, and sooner or later she will cut adrift from her present obligations and declare herself completely independent. It is fortunate for her that she can do that, whenever an opportunity occurs, without dishonouring her bond, which would not have been the case if England had accepted Mr. de Valera's pet—Document No. 2. For the Treaty as a treaty is only binding under the same conditions as any other treaty, i.e., so long as neither party desires to renounce it. It is not the Treaty we wanted and therefore we are not responsible for it. But if England had accepted Document No. 2, which was put forward as Ireland's proposal for a final settlement, we should be in honour bound to it so long as the British Empire existed.

No "settlement" of the Irish question is, or can be final, except separation from England.

In this connexion it may not be inapt to stress the point that the result of the civil war was not a defeat for separation any more than the victory of the Irregulars would have been a victory for separation. The Irregulars were no more fighting for a Republic than the National Army was fighting against it. The issue in the civil war was whether ordered democratic government was to obtain here, or whether we were to revert to Stone Age methods. It was government by ballot *versus* government by bullet, and in this instance the local Mussolinis were badly beaten.

Whether Ireland will survive at all, will depend, not on further political changes, but on the character and the institutions which she produces. And that is the gravest problem which confronts her.

In its forefront is the question of the revival of Irish, and it is the vital question. Ireland is a small nation of four millions, and she stands seventy miles from forty-five millions of English speakers on the east and a couple of thousand miles from a hundred and fifty millions of English speakers on the west, both of which communities are her nearest neighbours and those with whom she has the closest ties, economically and socially. If we do not revive and develop Irish, we must inevitably be assimilated by one of these two communities, or by the combined power which they must eventually form, and in that case our name and tradition and history will vanish out of human ken, and our national individuality will be lost. There is no disputing that, and no use in refusing to look it in the face. There is no case known to history where a nation retained its individuality, its separateness, once its language had been lost, and there are innumerable cases where a composite nation has adopted the language of one of its components and, with it, the culture and traditions of that one component, to the exclusion of the others.

The victory of 1921 was really a victory, not for any political party or political formula, but for the Irish language and culture, for what Douglas Hyde, thirty years ago, termed the de-anglicisation of Ireland. Thirty years of Gaelic League propaganda, though they have not succeeded in stopping to any material extent the decay in spoken Irish, have converted the nation as a whole to the principle of the Irish language. It is, unfortunately, true that the folly of the Irregulars has given the language movement a severe set-back, but that is only temporary; and there is no doubt that future Irish Governments will not alone continue, but extend as the country grows more normal, and as the financial position eases, the policy of safeguarding the Irish language, which the first Irish Government inaugurated, and gradually extending its use until it becomes of equal importance with English.

Of equal importance with that of the language is the question of the general character of the people; and that, unfortunately, is far from secure. On every side one finds disquieting happenings. One finds, after the wars and possibly because of them, no civic spirit, no patriotism, and a general moral and spiritual degeneration. Nothing has been more remarkable than the evidence which the last three years have brought that, as a nation, we have no real patriotism and that we are eaten up with class selfishness and materialism. When the Provisional Government was established it was at once subjected to what was practically blackmail by every section of the community. Every section wanted its wages raised, every section wanted taxation lowered, and every section threatened to strike, or to do something equally embarrassing to an inexperienced Government, unless its demands were at once acceded to. The civil service, pampered and overpaid, in enjoyment of the British scale of wages fixed by the British at the height of England's war prosperity, a scale which this country cannot afford to pay, blackmailed with the rest, and threw overboard, when they were dealing with an Irish Government, that tradition of service which they had maintained while they were dealing with an English one. Everywhere people started to form associations "to safeguard our interests"; everywhere groups and individuals began to push; nowhere was there any consideration for the country, any disposition to give the new Government a chance to survey the situation. I suppose it was

natural. I suppose that, as government has been for generations a thing apart from the people in Ireland—an enemy, a
thing which had the machinery for finding mysteriously
money from somewhere—it was too much to expect that
people would now recognise that this was *their* Government,
no longer an alien government, and that it could only find
money out of *their* own pockets. I suppose that it was natural,
seeing that for more than a century there has been no talk in
Ireland of anything but the people's rights, that now they
should forget that the people have any duties. But it was
none the less bitter to see in all Ireland no trace of that
decency, selflessness, and idealism, in which the movement
had been conceived and for many years carried on.

The same spirit manifested itself in the Dáil. The opposition
there was and is ineffective because it is based neither on
principle nor policy nor conviction. It is the most rigid and
selfish of Party or personal opposition, opposition for the sake
of opposition, opposition to good and bad alike. It has no
more thought for the good of the country as a whole, no more
notion of real patriotism, than have the mass of the people
themselves. The Senate, on the other hand, has done well. It
has developed a sense of real patriotism, and it does try to
look at things broadly and to consider the country as a whole
rather than Party or personal prejudice.

Apart from that, we have degenerated morally and spiritually.
The last years of the wars were years of moral unsettlement,
of which waves of loot and materialism were the result. There
has been a grave increase in sexual immorality, and a general
abandonment to levity and dissipation. Jazz dancing, the
motions and postures of which are ugly and ungainly, and
vary between suggestiveness and indecency, has swept Ireland
like a prairie fire. Bazaars, fetes, dances, crowd each other out,
and amusements and dissipation of all sorts flourish. Every
country in Europe had its riot of dissipation, I know, after the
war; but they could afford it, and I am not sure that we can.
They were, in a sense, already inoculated, whereas we were
not; and morally we have degenerated proportionately far
more than any of them. The atmosphere of materialism and

dissipation which we are developing is consistent neither with fine thinking, fine living, nor fine accomplishment.

If we are to have any future, it can only come to us through a development of character and through work. Our Budget balances on the wrong side, and our imports and exports balance on the wrong side. These will not be readjusted by substituting the Republic, or the Workers' Republic, or the Socialist Republic, or any other form of government, for the present one, but by hard work and honest dealing. There is no regeneration possible through sloth and license, but only through work and cleanliness.

The one hopeful augury is, curiously enough, the most belied and abused thing in the country—the present Government. It has never been given a chance; It has been given fair play neither by its friends nor its enemies. It has had a task which placed upon its chief members a strain which was almost inhuman. It has been subjected to calumny and misrepresentation, personal and collective, on a scale hitherto unknown amongst us. Yet it has governed, on the whole, justly and honestly and with integrity, doing the thing which it believed to be right notwithstanding popular disapproval. And it has pulled this nation out of the worst morass it ever was in. That we should have found, at the time and in the circumstances, a Government so capable, gives sure hope that whatever Government succeeds in new conditions will also rise to its responsibilities; and that in conditions of peace and under capable leadership the people as a whole will find themselves, and will re-erect in Ireland a civilisation and a polity which will redound to the nation's credit.

But if that is to come, there has got to be a change. We must get back to simplicity and strenuousness. Jazz dancing, joy rides, fetes, and bazaars have never built a civilisation, and never will build one. They lead only to fatty degeneration of the morals, of the character; to inefficiency and extinction. We may go out in a blaze of light, and music, and garishness, as Babylon went out, but unless we produce something other than a craze for idleness and amusement, we certainly shall go out. There is more in life than amusement, and as a people we must find that out. We must rediscover work and rediscover honesty. We must rediscover the Duties of Man, and bury the illusory Rights of Man deep down with the conception of Force as the arbiter of political quarrels. We must, above all, rediscover the Soul of Man, which we have fouled and bloodied and bruised. We must heal and cleanse and strengthen it by service, by honesty, by fine thinking and fine living. It is in the race to be fine and to be great. Only a nation with the elements of greatness in it would have come through what we have come through in the last five years. The people themselves are sound, but they want leadership—from the politicians, from the Church, from the artists, and from the men and women of good will. For various reasons they have not, up to now, had that leadership. *They must get it.* The men who lead, the men who think, must give that leadership. They must go back to that ideal of service and honesty without which nothing can be done; they must strip themselves free from every littleness and every unworthiness. Davis asked for "righteous men" and the need was never greater than it is now.

September, 1923—June, 1924.

APPENDIX I.

SOME PROPHECIES FULFILLED.

A

Should "Ulster" be Boycotted Economically?

When an English paper first made public the fact that the traders of Tuam had decided to boycott "Ulster," it seemed to me so incredible a thing that I gave no credence to the report until there came confirmation from this side. Surely, said I to myself, Sinn Féin will not countenance this; and I discussed the matter with all and sundry whom I happened to meet, including some Belfast Sinn Féiners. I was amazed to find a majority in favour of the boycott.

The bad example of Tuam has not, so far as I know, been generally followed, but as the matter is of considerable importance, it may be not inapt to set down what seems to me to be weighty reasons against any such policy as the policy of economic boycott.

Five years ago, or at any time previous, it would have been unnecessary to preach to advanced nationalism the text of Davis. From his time to our own the separatists have always built on the indivisibility of Ireland, on the inclusion in the Irish nation of all classes and all creeds. But Sinn Féin is at present suffering from having a majority who understand neither Sinn Féin nor nationalism, and who would bring it to wreck on the rocks on which the Irish Parliamentary Party almost brought Ireland to wreck. When Mr. Devlin, many years ago revived bigotry in Ireland by the reorganisation and extension of the Ancient Order of Hibernians, it seemed at the time a small matter, but its consequences were almost fatal. And equally so the spirit of the Tuam boycott, if it becomes in any way representative of Sinn Féin, will have equally deplorable consequences.

Separatist nationalism in Ireland has always been non-party, in the sense that it stood for the whole nation, that its philosophy was the philosophy which has been pregnantly expressed in Parnell's phrase "Ireland cannot do without the services of even a single Orangeman." That has been one of its great strengths. It has attracted to it the decent men and women of all classes and creeds who gave Ireland their first allegiance. It has been the spirit which was also mainly responsible for the vitality and success of the Gaelic League. Now that, from being a leavening minority, it has become an overwhelming majority in the nation, it must, to be true to itself, see that the nation shall be as broad and as free as were the foundations of its philosophy, and its fundamental principle is the principle of the essential unity of Ireland.

The Tuam boycott accepts Partition.

England's ease in Ulster is that in Ireland there are two nations, differing in language, race, outlook, traditions and interests. Our case is that in Ireland there is but one nation. And history supports our case. When England puts up "Ulster" as a national growth, history sees in it a myth invented by England and maintained by her. When Tuam proclaims an economic boycott against Ulster, when it proclaims that its natural interests are with the South rather than with its nearest trade centres, it accepts the theory that there is in Ulster a people differing radically from the rest of us. When it declares war on Sir Edward Carson as being the person who is denying Ireland freedom, it makes a fool of itself and plays England's game. Not "Ulster," but England, denies Ireland freedom: and England, not Ulster, is the enemy to be fought. The traders of Tuam might well turn their wrath from Belfast commercial travellers to English commercial travellers and English goods.

I am an old-fashioned Sinn Féiner. I believe in the principles of Davis, Mitchel, and Pearse, that "righteous men must make our land a nation once again," that the spirit is of far more importance than the letter, and that the men of "Ulster" are fools and not knaves. And I believe also that to turn the forces of the nation towards an economic boycott of a portion of the nation is to deny nationality.

If we have to fight "Ulster," let us fight her in the old honourable way, in all courtesy and with what weapons we have, as Cuchulain fought Ferdiadh, as the men of Ulster in the old days fought the men of the four-fifths of Ireland. But to fight with an economic boycott is to be as contemptible as the late Allies were when they fought with starvation. And it will only harden and give reality to "Ulster."

Sinn Féin, I think, should go into this boycott question and give a lead to the country before other unthinking traders follow Tuam's bad example.

(From *Old Ireland*, 21st February, 1920).

B

Ireland and America.

It would be a great mistake to count too much on America. The present leaders of Sinn Féin are much too gullible people in matters of that kind, much too fond of believing that cows afar off have long horns. When in the *Irish World* in the days of the Wilsonian ascendancy I pleaded for the maintenance towards him of a highly critical attitude, and adopted that attitude myself in examining his pronouncements and his record, I was almost denounced as an enemy to the Republic. Nevertheless I proved to be absolutely right in my analysis of the situation, and I would plead now for a similar reserve with regard to America generally. Public meetings are swayed by sentiment, by idealism, by principle, but the policy of nations never by anything except their own interest. America will do anything for Ireland except jeopardise an American interest. America will help Ireland so far as she can in furtherance of an American policy. America will no more go to war with England for the sake of freeing Ireland than she went to war with Germany for the sake of freeing Belgium and Servia. There are those in Ireland and in England who expect war between England and America within a few years; and it is in a frantic endeavours to prevent that that we see Sir Horace Plunkett amongst the prophets. But I think we would be unwise to count on that war, or to regard the present temper of America as being any more weighty hot air than the various ebullitions which occurred there between the war of 1812 and our own day. The present ferment is a political one, an election one, and when the Presidential election of November next is over, I do not think that there will be much more bellicosity. England and America may fight yet for the headship of the English-speaking world, but that time is not yet.

In the meantime we would do well to base our calculations mostly on what we can accomplish ourselves here in Ireland, and treat places outside Ireland as minor theatres— which really they are. Here in Ireland we have to solve the problem, and the Irish abroad can give us no more direct assistance than they were able to give at Easter Week. They help, indirectly, by the pressure they can bring to bear against English interests abroad, and also by cultivating their unrivalled opportunities for establishing outside Ireland a sympathetic international atmosphere. Their business, in fact, is propaganda and finance; ours is work. The Irish in America failed to prevent America going to war with Germany in order to save England from defeat; they will never induce America to go to war with England. Let us remember that. Embassies, and consuls, and foreign propaganda, and hot foreign air are all very well and very useful in their own way; but if an Irish Republic is to be established it will have to be established by us here, and whatever situation arises here will have to be dealt with by us here. Up to the present we have dealt with them stumblingly and accidentally. We shall have to deal with them with forethought.

We have won our fight so far because we have at last recognised that not all the world can govern Ireland against its will if it be really determined not to be governed. England governed us so long, not against our will, but with our assent. In words we objected, but in deeds we assented. But all machines of government depend for their existence on two things—upon those who work the machine and upon those who suffer it. In the past we both worked it and suffered it, and, therefore, although we went forth to do battle, we always fell. But when we withdrew our support from the sufferance of the machine as well as from the working of it, we beat England. And so long as we maintain that position England cannot beat us. Here in Ireland and by us here in Ireland alone, has that transformation been effected, and here in Ireland alone is it possible to maintain it. We have accomplished a complete mental revolution in the nation, and the giving actual physical expression to that mental revolution is a question of time and staying power. Germany could not help us. America cannot help us. We can help ourselves. We are helping ourselves. Let us go on doing it. If we remain firm England must, sooner or later, evacuate. She must come to terms—*our* terms. We have only to hold out.

(From *Old Ireland*, March 13th, 1920).

C

The Treaty.—First Aid to Politicians.

When I went out this morning, one of the first things that caught my eye was the poster of an English Sunday paper bearing the words, "Story of the Irish Split." That was, I hope, an unintelligent anticipation. There is yet no split in Ireland, and it behoves everyone in Ireland to see that there shall be no split. But certain things must be said.

(1) De Valera's action in issuing a Presidential *pronunciamento* on a question on which he could not carry his Cabinet seems to me to be wholly unconstitutional. In a case of that nature there are two constitutional courses either to resign and allow the Cabinet majority to form a Cabinet agreed on their policy, or else to dissolve Parliament altogether and appeal to the country. The course which has actually been adopted is unconstitutional, and is also unwise, as carrying with it the danger of a split. I give my voice against it.

(2) The Treaty is not, in many ways, a bad Treaty. In many ways it is a good Treaty. It has two objectionable provisions, viz., Partition and the oath of allegiance to the British Commonwealth.

(3) Partition is unavoidable. The English Liberals said that they would not coerce Ulster. So said the English Tories. So said English Labour—and so said de Valera. With everybody concerned agreed that Ulster should not be coerced, how is Ulster to be got in? When Dáil Eireann instituted the Belfast boycott, the most anti-national thing which has ever been done in Ireland by a representative nationalist body, it accepted and enforced Partition.

(4) The oath is objectionable. It is the real crux. But it is objectionable only because it implies association with the British Empire. In itself it is harmless, and as its primary allegiance is to the Irish Free State, it is as weak an oath as could be devised. *But* it was obvious from the beginning of the negotiations that an oath of allegiance or association would be the end of them. And this is an oath of association far more than it is an oath of allegiance.

(5) In the course of the last two years the Irish people have had one of their decadal attacks of ceasing to think politically. They handed over their thinking to the Dáil Eireann Cabinet. They became largely a herd manipulated by a machine. So did Dáil Eireann. It accepted everything it was told and did everything it was told.

When the negotiations began five months ago, and did not finish after de Valera's first meeting with Lloyd George, it was perfectly clear to anybody who did any independent thinking that the Republic was gone, and that we were negotiating on the basis of association with the British Empire. On no other basis could the negotiations have proceeded for more than one meeting. And whenever anything occurred which seemed to endanger that basis there was a "crisis." I do not care what assurances or explanations were given by the Dáil Cabinet: there is no excuse whatever for any member of the Dáil Eireann now to say that he never dreamed of a solution of associating Ireland with the British Empire. And there is less excuse for any member of the Dáil Cabinet. People who did not see that the Republic was gone, and that our Cabinet was negotiating on the association-with-the-British-Empire basis, either did not want to see or were totally unfitted to take political responsibilities. In the whole of the correspondence the Irish Republic was only mentioned by de Valera to assure Lloyd George that we were not asking England to recognise it, as a preliminary, either formally or informally; while when the first British terms were published the *Irish Bulletin* attacked them, not because they did not concede Ireland independence, but because while offering Dominion status they did not really give it.

(6) Let, therefore, no member of Dáil Eireann, Cabinet or otherwise, say now that he did not know what was being done. It was plain before his face in the public Press several times a week if he troubled to read the correspondence without preconception.

(7) Once the negotiations had become established the country as a whole assumed that it was peace. Every day they lasted strengthened that opinion. It would have been impossible, in my judgment, to get it back to the war spirit again as unitedly and as wholeheartedly as it was in the pre-negotiation days.

(8) Now, after a Treaty has been concluded and signed, after a considerable body of honest opinion has declared for its ratification, there is no question of the resumption of war. We have not the united will which alone could justify and sustain it.

(9) If there be any members of Dáil Eireann who have opposed these negotiations since the beginning, opposed them because they could only lead to compromise, they are entitled to oppose the ratification of the Treaty to which they led. But no other member of Dáil Eireann is entitled to do that. Their business is to take the responsibility for what they have done, as Griffith and Collins have, and not to try and save their faces by belated heroics. Let them not try to shift the responsibility elsewhere. Except those, if any, who opposed, and those *(e.g.,* Dr. MacCartan) who were away, they are all equally responsible.

(10) This Treaty will not settle the Irish question. Her destiny is to be an independent nation, not a member, associated or otherwise, of any Empire. The Irish Republican Brotherhood, which has been the political sheet anchor of Ireland since Stephens founded it more than sixty years ago, will go on.

December 11th, 1921.

(From *New Ireland*, December 17th, 1921).

D

The Decision.

Dáil Eireann, by a majority of seven votes in a poll of 121, has decided to ratify the Treaty. That that decision represents the will of the people of Ireland as a whole, at the present moment, we have no doubt, much though we regret it. But we have equally no doubt that the ratification does not represent an abandonment, either by the Dáil majority or the majority of the people, of the Republic. We all want independence, independence total and complete, without association either internal or external with the British Empire. Collins and Griffith want that as much as de Valera and Brugha, and the people as a whole want it. But they equally clearly wanted this Treaty ratified. It is idle now to go into the question of who is or was responsible for the mess into which the Republican movement slid in the last six months. We hold that they were all, either by sins of commission or of omission, responsible— President, Cabinet, and Dáil; that they created, or allowed to be created under their very eyes, a situation which made the maintenance of the demand for independence impossible at the moment, which made the ratification of the Treaty the only thing to be done now. But that ends that. The future is with the Separatists.

We do not know whether anybody in Ireland or outside it regards this as settling the Irish question. Very few in Ireland, we should imagine, do so regard it: but there may be some outside Ireland who do. But that is impossible. There can be only one settlement, one real peace, in Ireland, and that is separation. Ireland is no colony, no new people, no conglomeration of breeds, but a nation, an ancient nation with a memory as long and as clean as any other European nation, with all a nation's will and courage and characteristics. Nothing on earth can make the British Empire otherwise than loathsome to us, and nothing on earth but duress will keep us in it, or in association with it. That sort of thing is all very well for Canada and Australia, where the population is predominantly English, and there is a case for it in South Africa, where the English population, in the Union as a whole, is so large. But in Ireland, where the anti-Irish minority is small, where there is a living and vital national tradition to hold to, there is only one possible end to the struggle, and that is independence.

What the leaders on both sides have to do now is to take stock. We have to begin by recognising that the separatist movement, as a whole, has suffered a check. As against this Treaty, the nation, as a whole, would not now fight for a Republic. It would prefer a Republic, but it would not fight for it, as it thinks that the Treaty gives it something which it can stand on and breathe awhile, pending a fresh effort. But be that as it may, we are back again where we were years ago, a separatist minority, this time under an Irish Government instead of under an English Government, which makes the position somewhat more difficult. But that is the fact we have to face. And we hope that the leaders on both sides will face it in cold blood, without passion or prejudice, and, above all, without too much self-righteousness *and without any bitterness either of word or of act towards each other.* The personal bitterness displayed in the Dáil debate, the personal attacks made, the attempt to load the responsibility for the situation on to this or that group or individual, we condemn wholeheartedly. They were all responsible. They are all responsible. They are all faced now with the wreck of the movement which they led up to six months ago, and upon them all is the responsibility of mending that wreck. Bitter talk, bitter deeds, bitter hearts, will not mend it, nor will they help Ireland. But it can be mended by honesty and charity and by no rushing at hasty decisions. It must be mended if the nation is to be saved. It must be recognised that all parties concerned acted in good faith, and were equally the victims of their common failure to see where they were going. If that be not admitted—if we are to have a bitter split, punctuated by the familiar charges and epithets—then God help Ireland.

We stand, at any rate, in the Ireland of to-morrow, as of yesterday, for separation, for the Republic. But in doing so, we decline to join in. Let all that rest. It will not mend matters. Let us all think, instead, of what we can do now. The any cry against the men who backed this Treaty. Future is with us. For a while the present was ours, and with it we did wonders. We have to work so that it shall be with us again.

And let no man say that the Republic is dead. Its life is neither in Dáil Eireann nor in the I.R.A., but in the spirit and the will of the Irish people. And these, ultimately, we are always sure of.

(From *New Ireland*, 14th January, 1922).

E

De Valera's Road to Ruin.

We desire to write as temperately as possible about the incitements to civil war and worse which Mr. de Valera and some of his supporters delivered at the week end. Elsewhere on this page we give the threat used by Mr. de Valera on St. Patrick's Day, a threat which he repeated two days afterwards, on the 19th. So that, whatever it may mean in his own mind, it is not a thing which he said in impulse, or in temper, but a calculated statement of policy. As it stands, there can be no two opinions about its meaning. It is a threat and an incitement: a threat to the voters who listened to him that unless they vote for his party at the elections, he will plunge this country into civil war, and wade through the blood of his opponents; and an incitement to his own followers to civil war, and worse; a call for salvation by blood.

We, at any rate, unassociated separatists, condemn unreservedly a speech and a temper which are unpatriotic and unsocial and unmoral, and which lead nowhere but to ruin. Had it been a single speech, allowances might be made for it, but the same bloody sentiment, the same bloody incitement was repeated in cold blood after the interval of one day after its first launching. It remains, therefore, a statement of policy. In a speech delivered on the same day in another place, Mr. MacEntee threatened that the Volunteers would "sweep away" Mr. Griffith. It is, evidently, the policy which is running through the mind of the Anti-Treaty Party. It is the complete road to ruin.

There is one possible defence of this policy, and that is the defence which Mr. Brugha made last week of a somewhat similar, if less precise, utterance, and that is that it is a warning, not an incitement. Mr. de Valera may think that in the event of the Treaty being ratified at the elections there will remain no way of obtaining unassociated independence but through the blood of Collins, Griffith, Mulcahy, and those who stand for the Treaty, and he may think that he is only trying to make clear to the average voter what the consequences of voting against the Anti-Treaty Party will be.

If it were a different thing, that might hold. If he said, "Pass this Treaty and you make it more difficult than ever to obtain for Ireland unassociated independence," then the plea of the warning voice might be a tenable plea. But as things are, it is not a tenable plea; for it is couched as a threat other than as a warning. "Pass the Treaty and we wade through blood." That is it, bluntly. It is a threat and an incitement. It is an indication of the line their reasoning is taking, an anticipation of events which they mean to compass. Mr. Brugha said recently that he had said long ago that he and de Valera were against the Treaty because it would not bring peace, and, he added, it will not bring peace.

Why not? Because they determined that it should not bring peace. If the Treaty does not bring peace, the main reason is that those who prophesied that it would not, busied themselves in crucifying peace and in making certain, as far as they could make certain, that it would not bring peace. When they said, "This will not bring peace," it meant "We will crucify peace." And when they say now that if the Treaty is passed there will be no way to freedom save over the bodies of Griffith and Collins and Mulcahy, and their followers, it means, not that there is no other way, but that they mean to try that way. It means the demon of Party, which ever since he fell from grace, has been invading Mr. de Valera, has so completely gained possession of him that his spiritual ego is completely overthrown, drowned in passion and in dreams of blood.

It is not true that that is the only way. It is not true that, under the Treaty, Ireland will lose her soul or her manhood. It is true that she *can* be, under it, stronger, more Irish, more independent, than ever she has been, if her government is worked by the right people and in the right way, and to the right end. And it is equally true that the way pointed out by Mr. de Valera is not only not the only way, but it is not a way. It does not lead to freedom, but to murder and anarchy, not to Heaven but to hell.

(From *The Separatist*, 25th March, 1922).

F

The Political Army.

On the 26th March, the O'Connor wing of the I.R.A. held its Convention, and at that Convention they are reported to have come to a number of decisions. One decision, to which their own official report committed them, was the decision to reimpose and strengthen the boycott of Belfast. Singled out for special and only mention in the report, it was clearly the star turn, the thing that was to demonstrate to Ireland that this was the real true-blue republicanism, and not the associated variety. And that marked the O'Connor army definitely and clearly as a political army. The question of an economic boycott is essentially a civilian question, a political question, a question for a government and not for a G.H.Q., and interference by an army in a political question of that sort is political interference; it is taking sides, it is substituting the .45 for the ballot box. It alone demonstrated that whoever was at the Convention, the politicians had the votes.

Now mark it in operation. The decision to boycott Belfast was come to on the 26th March. Day by day we waited for the promised full report of the proceedings, but it never appeared. Then, on the morning of the 31st March was published the news and details of the agreement which had been come to by Griffith, Collins, and Craig. It was a nasty blow to the O'Connor wing. Here were they, doing their best to turn to account the madness of Belfast, doing their best to make political capital, Party capital, out of the existence in Belfast of a savage mental area, and here was a thing which threatened to deprive them of their cherished political capital. Well, they simply went on with their insensate proposal. On the day after the publication of the Collins-Griffith-Craig agreement, appeared the solemn proclamation reimposing the boycott. It was dated 31st March. That is to say, on reading the morning paper containing the news that peace in Ireland had been agreed to, Messrs. O'Connor and Co. sat down and crucified peace. There shall be no peace, decreed they, and straight away they framed and published their proclamation, which reimposes, in so far as they can reimpose it, what is to Ireland's dishonour ever to have imposed, and which leads, not to peace in Belfast or peace in Ireland, not to unity in Ireland nor to safety for the Nationalists, but to death and murder and savagery. For the old Belfast boycott was more responsible for what happened in Belfast than anyone down here cares to admit.

Consider the callousness of it. Here was at the least, a chance for the minority in the six counties. Here was a chance that peace might be secured to them, and security. Here was a definite agreement, with safeguards and provisions, and with a proviso also that the way to unity in Ireland should remain open. Ordinary decency, to say nothing of patriotism, demanded that the thing should be given a trial. But that would not do. You see, it might succeed, it might bring peace, and then where would be the looked-for political capital? So the irresponsibles proceeded to do their best to ensure that it should not bring peace, should not succeed. They stuck into the still quivering sore in Ulster the bayonet, poisoned with boycott virus—not a clean cut, not a decent wound, but the most ignoble weapon of hate and devilishness that the degenerate mind of man has evolved, the economic weapon. And now they are waiting for results. Having done their utmost to split Ireland, they go around prating about their ability to give Ireland peace and unity, when they have nothing for her but the tyranny of force—the sledgehammer, the gun, the black-and-tannery that they have borrowed from the English. Mr. O'Connor suppressed the *Freeman's Journal* because it "encouraged disaffection in the army." Oh, yes; we have heard that before. It was the reason alleged when the *Irish Volunteer, Irish Freedom, The Spark, Honesty, The Gael, Sinn Féin, Eire, Scissors and Paste, Nationality, An Saoghal Gaedhealach,* and *New Ireland* were suppressed by Mr. O'Connor's predecessors. It was the reason alleged when provincial printing machinery was dismantled by Mr. O'Connor's predecessors. It is always the tyrant's reason. When he finds that he cannot subdue mind he sees red, and when he sees red he is never at a loss for a good moral reason for devilishness. *That,* we used to regard as a special English characteristic. It isn't. It is probably a part of general human nature. And, as the foundations of society and of sanity break up here, there gradually emerges nothing but the primitive and brutal brute.

We are getting back to the savage. When Mr. de Valera puts it up as a necessary thing to wade through Irish blood, he is not acting the bogey man: he is merely demonstrating that, fundamentally, he too is nothing but a savage with a thin veneer of civilisation, and that once he breaks up in his own mind the mould of order, of social responsibility, upon which ultimately western civilisation hangs, he becomes an unreasoning savage, with nothing left save the primitive impulses of ferocity and pugnacity and selfishness. And that he and Mr. O'Connor can say and do the things they say and do, and find support to the extent to which they do find it, is merely an indication that all of us are savage, and that the whole of our civilisation is only a veneer, a thing of custom, of convention, hardly more than skin deep. And when the hurlers on the ditch, the people who when the war was on remained steadily above the battle and trembled when an explosion came anywhere near their precincts, when these now become atavistic warriors, when their pens, which during the war trod the careful ways of peace, become suddenly warlike, become suddenly vitriolically vilificatory, it is not that they have suddenly gone mad: it is only that the general sapping of the foundations has let loose in them too that strange lust for blood, that strange thirst for violence, that sudden emergence of the primitive brute, which comes to a people when anarchy also comes.

And anarchy is coming. Let nobody doubt it. Already, see you, it is showing its fangs, its great cruel upper lip curling over them. Already, see you, its eyes are beginning to gloat, for it is going to have a royal time. Already, see you, it feels the call of its hour, it feels the emergence in the hearts of men of everything base, everything ignoble, everything petty, everything unclean. Already it feels that here is a mass of people about to be possessed by devils, devils who will possess and devour them. And it gloats, and it waits.

"Righteous men," wrote Davis, "must make our land a nation once again." He was wrong. There are no righteous men. There are only unreasoning, bloodthirsty savages, truculent swaggering men, and women with serpents' tongues—poisonous tongues. From the darkness which rapidly closes over this island they laugh and jeer and go about their dreadful business, their true likenesses coming out in this hour of the emergence of the real ego. And the primary characteristic is evil, evil. Here is evil, sinister, gloating, triumphant, lit up by the red flames of hell, here it is steadily gaining on us, steadily digging itself in in our consciousness, steadily gaining the upper hand. It is the last scene of all, the worst scene of all for the human soul, when Hyde finally ousts Jekyll. That is where we are. We, that used to be Jekyll, that thought ourselves to be the only genuine Jekyll, find out that we are only Hyde after all, find out what all the philosophers have known and what all the theologians have known, that there is no such person as Jekyll. Jekyll is merely auto-suggestion, and has no genuine existence. Hyde is the foundation and the reality, and we are almost all Hyde now. With great words, and passions, and gestures, with much insistence on what ought to have been done, and what ought to have been agreed to; with much mutual vilification, our great men pursue the de-Jekyllisation of Ireland, and with success. In thirty years of hard struggle a beginning was made in the work of de-Anglicisation in Ireland. And it was begun, the fates saw to it, by a Jekyll who was named Hyde. But in three months Ireland has been almost de-Jekyllised by our Jekyll who was named Jekyll but who really was Hyde. Thus the gods pursue mankind with laughter, and whip them with scorpions.

Evil stalks this land. It talks about freedom and suppresses it: it talks about peace and crucifies it: it talks about unity and boycotts it: it talks about the will of the people and tramples on it. It has no longer any sanity, any generosity, any brotherliness—it is possessed by Devils.

(From *The Separatist*, 15th April, 1922).

G

The Weakness of Democracy.

"We all believe in Democracy, but we do not forget its well-known weaknesses."—Mr. de Valera, in the *Chicago Tribune*, May 15th.

"Touching what you say about liberty of conscience, I meddle with no man's conscience, but if by liberty of conscience you mean liberty to exercise the Mass, then I tell you that where the Parliament of England hath power there that will not be allowed."—Oliver Cromwell at Kilkenny.

"There is no peace, but smothered war. . . ."—Hussey de Burgh, 1782.

We could wish that Mr. de Valera were as outspoken as Cromwell, or as courageous as Lenin and Trotsky. They, too, discovered the weaknesses of democracy, but they didn't pretend to believe in it while they were crushing it. The Bolsheviks have been quite frank about democracy. Under any sort of democratic constitution it is impossible for a minority of a people to impose their will on the majority. The Bolsheviks were in the position of being a minority who wished to impose their will on the majority. They could only do that by force. They did it by force. They could only do it by throwing over democracy as a principle of government. They did throw it overboard. If democracy will not allow us to rule Russia against the wishes of the people of Russia, democracy does not work and must be replaced, said they. It is an understandable position. But they did not pretend to believe in democracy, any more than Cromwell pretended to believe in the Mass.

The weakness of democracy is, of course, well known. It is that in a democratic constitution, the clearly-expressed will of the people, must prevail, and must be given effect to irre-spective of the amount of war material in the hands of any one political party. To most of us that is democracy's strength, and twelve months ago Mr. de Valera was acclaiming it. He stood, then, on Ireland's moral right, and he proclaimed that moral right against all the physical force which England could bring to bear against it. Now that strength has become a weakness! Why? Because the majority of the people no longer agree with Mr. de Valera.

The acid test of everything for Mr. de Valera, is whether he can win on it or whether he can not. None of the principles or theories which he enunciates mean anything whatever to him except so many means of helping him to get his own way. So long as they help him to do that they are admirable, but when they cease to do that, when they become in any way inconvenient, they go overboard, just as the Republic did in July last. It is the test of the political opportunist, to whom politics are nothing but a game, and who messes about with principles that do mean something to other men, and messes about with questions of life and death, with no realisation whatever of the gravity of the situation with which he is faced. Mr. de Valera has thrown over the Irish people, and Dáil Eireann, and the principle of democracy, because he cannot win on them. He supports the principle of military tyranny, because on that he thinks he can win. But when the civil war is over, he will call the army infamous if the pro-Treaty section of it wins.

The point at issue now is not, as Mr. de Valera so glibly puts it, a question of dishonour or disaster. It is not whether the Treaty is to be put into operation or not. But it is whether the will of the people is to prevail over the anti-social, anti-national policy of military tyranny, and it is a point which Ireland must settle or perish. It is a point which she will settle, for otherwise life will grow intolerable and savage. It is growing intolerable and savage. If the principle be conceded by this country that a minority of its people, because they happen to have arms, are to be allowed to impose their will on the people as a whole, there is an end to all order and government in Ireland.

"We know the people of Ireland do not want to forswear the independence they have declared." If that has any practical meaning, as apart from a propagandist meaning, it means that Mr. de Valera knows that the people of Ireland do not want the Treaty. Very well. How does he know? There is only one way of finding out whether they do or they don't, and that is to ask them—and that is the only thing Mr. de Valera is afraid of. He has used every possible political device to prevent them being asked, because he knows perfectly well that they do want the Treaty to be put into operation. It is dishonest to suggest that they don't. All this humbug in the *Chicago Tribune* means merely this, that the only support Mr. de Valera has against the will of the people is the tyranny of the Anti-Treaty army, and that, therefore, he supports that against democracy.

There is another army, a Pro-Treaty army, and if one army is going to maintain the position that it will not allow the people to decide this question by ordinary democratic procedure, the other army will take up the position that the first army has got to be eliminated. And that is the point at which we have arrived—powder and shot the sole nexus as between man and man, as Carlyle would put it. If the Anti-Treatyites go on spurning democracy, and brandishing the sword against Everyman, Everyman will get him a sword too and will use it. These things are incredible, think you? Maybe they are, but they will happen unless this attempt to establish in Ireland a military tyranny is dropped. And it won't be dropped, because it is the only possible way in which the Anti-Treaty Party can win. And what they are concerned about is not the country, but winning their political corner.

Meantime the country generally is being driven into a definite embracing of the Treaty, and what happened last week in Dublin is significant on that point. The Lord Mayor of Dublin, playing the innocent, refused to recognise the Provisional Government, alleging that he only recognised Dáil Eireann, and refusing to take cognisance of the fact that the Provisional Government is Dáil Eireann. At a meeting of the Dublin Corporation it was proposed that the Provisional Government be recognised, and it was proposed as an amendment that Dáil only be recognised. The amendment was defeated by a three to one majority.

That is what Everyman is coming to think.

(From *The Separatist*, 20th May, 1922).

APPENDIX II.

MR. LIAM LYNCH'S FIRST FRIGHTFULNESS ORDER.

*Extract from Report of Inquest on Hugh Houghton
of Dublin.*

A Colonel *in* the National Army said he had joined the
Volunteers in January, 1917, and had been on the Adjt.-
General's Staff since July, 1920. He knew the previous witness
since 1917. He was one of the most active members in Dublin,
and had a record any Irishman could be proud of. He identified
the signature on a captured document produced as that of
Liam Lynch, Chief of Staff in the Irregular Army. The document was as follows:

*"Irish Republican Army,
"G.H.Q., Dublin.
"Operation Order No. 11,
"Nov. 30, 1922.*

"To O.C. all Divs.

"Enemy Murder Bill.

"1. All members of P.G. Parliament who were present and
voted for Murder Bill to be shot at sight. Attached find list of
same.

"2. Houses of supporters of Murder Bill, Murder Gang, and
active supporters of P.G. who are known to support Murder
Bill decision will be destroyed.

"3. All F. S. Army Officers who approve of Murder Bill,
and are aggressive and active against our forces, will be shot
at sight, also all ex-British Army Officers and men who joined
F. S. Army since Dec. 6, 1921.

"4. Individual action on paragraphs 2, 3 will be ordered by
Bde. O.C.

"5. To be duplicated to Bde. and Bn. O.C.s and transmitted to O.C.'s all units.

"LIAM LYNCH, Chief of Staff.

"Note.—On the day of first executions an order to shoot at sight members of P.G. was issued to Dublin No.1/2 Brigades. Since an opportunity was not got to put same into effect.—C.S."

(From *Independent*, 15th March, 1923).

B

MR. LIAM LYNCH'S LAST FRIGHTFULNESS ORDER.

The following captured document, found in the course of a raid in Dublin, was released for publication by G.H.Q.:—

"Brigade Headquarters, Dublin.

"To O.C. Battalion III.

"1. To meet the desperate and more barbarous methods being adopted by the enemy to destroy the Government and Army of the Republic, G.H.Q. has decided to amend and make more drastic in some cases the action ordered in recent Operation and General Orders, orders to Commandants.

"Some of these orders have been cancelled, and the action ordered in them embodied in a new order, which will come into operation if any further executions by the enemy are carried out in this area after this date.

"It is the declared intention of the enemy to execute all members of the Army Council Executive, or senior officers prisoners in their hands. In the meantime the existing orders continue in force.

"2. The portions of the new order that effect this Brigade are as follows:—

"(a) The recent order for special destruction of houses for future executions should they occur will be strictly carried out within as few hours as possible after the executions. Owners will be informed verbally of the reason for destruction and the special execution for which the particular destruction is being carried out.

"(b) The following enemies of the Republic will be shot at sight:—

"(1) All members of the F. S. Parliament who voted for or support the policy of the F. S. Government in executing Republican prisoners of war.

"(2) Officers of all ranks of the enemy army.

"(3) Members of the Senate under category 'A' on list which accompanies Operation Order No. 16, *i.e.,* for this area, Senators John Bagwell and A. Jameson.

"(4) Members of the Murder Gang.

"(5) Officials (civilians) who order prisoners to be fired on.

"(6) Persons who are guilty of torturing Republican prisoners.

"(7) Enemy troops of any rank who fire on prisoners.

"(8) Enemy legal advisers connected with courtmartials or committees for 'Trial' and sentence of prisoners of war.

"(9) Members of firing parties who execute prisoners of war.

"(10) Judges and solicitors exercising jurisdiction under the authority of the F.S. Government, that is: High Court, County and District Judges, and State Solicitors.

"(11) Officials (civilian or military) employed at the headquarters of the different enemy Ministries.

"(12) Aggressive civilian supporters of the Free State Government policy of executions of prisoners of war, that is: persons who openly advocate or defend such executions.

"(13) Members of the C.I.D.

"(14) Proprietors, directors, of hostile Press in Ireland and senior officials employed in same, such as editors, sub-editors, leader writers in cases where these officials are known to be hostile.

"(c) The residences, and where mentioned the offices, of the following shall be destroyed, if the property of the persons named:—

"Note.—Factories are in no case to be destroyed.

"(1) Houses of persons mentioned in Categories 1, 2, 4, 5, 6, 7, 8, 9, 10, also their offices 11, 12, 13, 14, of paragraph (b) of above.

"(2) Residences of all Senators.

"(3) Imperialists, such as late Privy Councillor, Deputy Lieutenants and those who stand for and represent the English interest in Ireland, particularly those who were active enemies of Ireland during the English occupation.

"(4) Officials connected with the enemy Government administration not provided above.

"(5) Counsels, barristers, solicitors, who appear in suits or actions before enemy courts without a permit from the Minister of Home Affairs, Irish Republican Government.

"3. I will as soon as possible issue a list of persons affected by these orders.

"You will also proceed immediately to compile a list as regards your area and let me have a copy to compare with or add to my lists.

"O.C. BRIGADE."

(From *Freeman's Journal*, 16th March, 1923).

APPENDIX III.

MR. DE VALERA'S FIRST THOUGHTS.

The following is the original version of Document No. 2, *i.e.,* the version which Mr. de Valera circulated to the Dáil in the first week of the Treaty debate, and which at the end of a week he withdrew. All Deputies were asked to hand in their copies of this document, so that it should leave no "footprints in the sands of time." But some copies survived.

It was for this precious document, and not for any of the revised versions or for "the existing Republic," that Mr. de Valera made the split and drenched Ireland in blood:—

DOCUMENT NO. 2.

Proposed Treaty of Association between Ireland and the British Commonwealth.

Preamble

In order to bring to an end the long and ruinous conflict between Great Britain and Ireland by a sure and lasting peace honourable to both nations, it is agreed

1. That the legislative, executive, and judicial authority of Ireland shall be derived solely from the people of Ireland.

2. That, for purposes of common concern, Ireland shall be associated with the States of the British Commonwealth, viz.: the Kingdom of Great Britain, the Dominion of Canada, the Commonwealth of Australia, the Dominion of New Zealand, and the Union of South Africa.

3. That when acting as an associate the rights, status, and privileges of Ireland shall be in no respect less than those enjoyed by any of the component States of the British Commonwealth.

4. That the matters of "common concern" shall include Defence, Peace and War, Political Treaties, and all matters now treated as of common concern among the States of the British Commonwealth, and that in these matters there shall be between Ireland and the States of the British Commonwealth "such concerted action founded on consultation as the several Governments may determine."

5. That in virtue of this association of Ireland with the States of the British Commonwealth citizens of Ireland in any of these States shall not be subject to any disabilities which a citizen of one of the component States of the British Commonwealth would not be subject to, and reciprocally for citizens of these States in Ireland.

6. That for purposes of the Association, Ireland shall recognise his Britannic Majesty as head of the Association.

7. That, so far as her resources permit, Ireland shall provide for her own defence by sea, land, and air, and shall repel by force any attempt by a foreign Power to violate the integrity of her soil and territorial waters, or to use them for any purpose hostile to Great Britain and the other associated States.

8. That for five years, pending the establishment of Irish coastal defence forces, or for such other period as the Governments of the two countries may later agree upon, facilities for the coastal defence of Ireland shall be given to the British Government as follows:—

> (a) In time of peace such harbour and other facilities as are indicated in the Annex hereto or such other facilities as may from time to time be agreed upon between the British Government and the Government of Ireland.

> (b) In time of war such harbour and other naval facilities as the British Government may reasonably require for the purposes of such defence as aforesaid.

9. That within five years from the date of exchange of ratifications of this Treaty a conference between the British and Irish Governments shall be held in order to hand over the coastal defence of Ireland to the Irish Government, unless some other arrangement for naval defence be agreed by both Governments to be desirable in the common interest of Ireland, Great Britain and the other associated States.

10. That, in order to co-operate in furthering the principle of international limitation of armaments, the Government of Ireland shall not

(a) Build submarines unless by agreement with Great Britain and the other States of the Commonwealth.

(b) Maintain a military defence force, the establishments whereof exceed in size such proportion of the military establishments maintained in Great Britain as that which the population of Ireland bears to the population of Great Britain.

11. That the Governments of Great Britain and Ireland shall make a convention for the regulation of civil communication by air.

12. That the ports of Great Britain and of Ireland shall be freely open to the ships of each country on payment of the customary port and other dues.

13. That Ireland shall assume liability for such share of the present public debt of Great Britain and Ireland and of the payment of war pensions as existing at this date as may be fair and equitable, having regard to any just claims on the part of Ireland by way of set-off or counter-claim, the amount of such sums being determined, in default of agreement, by the arbitration of one or more independent persons being citizens of Ireland or of the British Commonwealth.

14. That the Government of Ireland agrees to pay compensation on terms not less favourable than those proposed by the British Government of Ireland Act of 1920 to that Government's judges, officials, members of Police Forces and other Public Servants who are discharged by the Government of Ireland or who retire in consequence of the change of Government effected in pursuance hereof.

Provided that this agreement shall not apply to members of the Auxiliary Police Force or to persons recruited in Great Britain for the Royal Irish Constabulary during the two years next preceding the date hereof. The British Government will assume responsibility for such compensation or pensions as may be payable to any of these excepted persons.

15. That neither the Parliament of Ireland nor any subordinate legislature in Ireland shall make any law so as either directly or indirectly to endow any religion, or prohibit or restrict the free exercise thereof or give any preference or impose any disability on account of religious belief or religious status, or affect prejudicially the right of any child to attend a school receiving public money without attending the religious instruction at the school, or make any discrimination as respects State aid between schools under the management of different religious denominations, or divert from any religious denomination or any educational institution any of its property except for public utility purposes and on payment of compensation.

16. That by way of transitional arrangement for the administration of Ireland during the interval which must elapse between the date hereof and the setting up of a Parliament and Government of Ireland in accordance herewith, the members elected for constituencies in Ireland since the passing of the Government of Ireland Act in 1920 shall, at a meeting summoned for the purpose, elect a transitional Government, to which the British Government and Dáil Eireann shall transfer the authority, powers, and machinery requisite for the discharge of its duties, provided that every member of such transitional Government shall have signified in writing his or her acceptance of this instrument. But this arrangement shall not continue in force beyond the expiration of twelve months from the date hereof.

17. That without recognising the right of any part of Ireland to be excluded from the supreme authority of the National Parliament and Government, nevertheless in severe regard for internal peace, and in the desire to bring no force or coercion to bear upon any substantial part of the Province of Ulster whose inhabitants may now be opposed to the

acceptance of the National Authority, the following provisions shall have effect in the case of that portion of Ulster which is defined as "Northern Ireland" in the British Government of Ireland Act, 1920.

18. Until the expiration of one month from the passing of the Act of Parliament for the ratification of this instrument, the Powers of the Parliament and the Government of Ireland shall not be exercisable as respects Northern Ireland, and the provisions of the British Government of Ireland Act, 1920, shall, so far as they relate to Northern Ireland, have full force and effect; but no election shall be held for the return of members to serve in the Parliament of Ireland for constituencies in Northern Ireland unless a resolution is passed by both houses of Northern Ireland in favour of the holding of such elections before the end of the said month.

19. If, before the expiration of the said month, an address is presented to his Majesty by both Houses of the Parliament of Northern Ireland to that effect, the powers of the Parliament and the Government of Ireland shall no longer extend to Northern Ireland, and the provisions of the British Government of Ireland Act, 1920, (including those relating to the Council of Ireland), shall so far as they relate to Northern Ireland, continue to be of full force and effect, and this instrument shall have effect subject to the necessary modifications.

Provided that if such an address is so presented, a Commission consisting of three persons, one to be appointed by the Government of Ireland, one to be appointed by the Government of Northern Ireland, and one, who shall be Chairman, to be appointed by the British Government, shall determine in accordance with the wishes of the inhabitants, so far as may be compatible with economic and geographic conditions, the boundaries between Northern Ireland and the rest of Ireland, and for the purpose of the British Government of Ireland Act, 1920, and of this instrument, the boundary of Northern Ireland shall be such as may be determined by such Commission.

20. For the purpose of the last foregoing Article the power of the Parliament defined as the Parliament of Southern

Ireland under the British Government of Ireland Act, 1920, to elect members of the Council of Ireland, shall be exercised by the Parliament of Ireland.

21. After the expiration of the said month, if no such address as is mentioned in Article 19 hereof is presented, the Parliament and Government of Northern Ireland shall continue to exercise as respects Northern Ireland the powers conferred on them by the British Government of Ireland Act, 1920, but the Parliament and Government of Ireland shall in Northern Ireland have in relation to matters in respect of which the Parliament of Northern Ireland has not power to make laws under that Act, (including matters which under the said Act are within the jurisdiction of the Council of Ireland), the same powers as in the rest of Ireland subject to such other conditions as may be agreed in manner hereinafter appearing.

22. At any time after the date hereof the Government of Northern Ireland and the transitional Government of Ireland provided for in Article 16, may meet for the purpose of discussing the provisions subject to which the last foregoing Article is to operate in the event of no such address as is therein mentioned being presented, and those provisions may include:—

(a) Safeguards with regard to patronage in Northern Ireland;

(b) Safeguards with relation to the collection of Revenue in Northern Ireland;

(c) Safeguards with regard to import and export duties affecting the trade or industry of Northern Ireland;

(d) Safeguards for minorities in Northern Ireland;

(e) The settlement of the financial relations between Northern Ireland and Ireland.

(f) The establishment and powers of a local Militia in Northern Ireland and the relation of the Defence Forces of Ireland and of Northern Ireland respectively; and if at any such meeting provisions are agreed to, the same shall have effect as if it were included amongst the provisions subject to which the powers of the Parliament and the Government of Ireland are to be exercisable in Northern Ireland under Article 21 hereof.

23. That this instrument shall be submitted forthwith by his Britannic Majesty's Government for the approval of the Parliament at Westminster and by the Cabinet of Dáil Eireann to a meeting of the Members elected for the Constituencies in Ireland set forth in the British Government of Ireland Act, 1920, and if approved, shall be ratified by the necessary legislation.

THE ANNEX.

1. The following are the specific facilities referred to in Article 8 (a):—

Dockyard Port at Berehaven.—*(a)* British Admiralty property and rights to be retained as at the date hereof. Harbour defences to remain in charge of British care and maintenance parties.

Queenstown.—(b) Harbour defences to remain in charge of British care and maintenance parties. Certain mooring buoys to be retained for use of his Britannic Majestys' ships.

Belfast Lough.—(c) Harbour defences to remain in charge of British care and maintenance parties.

Lough Swilly.—(d) Harbour defences to remain in charge of British care and maintenance parties.

Aviation.—(e) Facilities in the neighbourhood of the above ports for coastal defence by air.

Oil Fuel storage.—(f) Haulbowline and Rathmullen—To be offered for sale to commercial companies under guarantee that purchasers shall maintain a certain minimum stock for British Admiralty purposes.

2. A Convention covering a period of five years shall be made between the British and Irish Governments to give effect to the following conditions

(a) That submarine cables shall not be landed or wireless stations for communication with places outside Ireland be established except by agreement with the British Government; that the existing cable landing rights and wireless concessions shall not be withdrawn except by agreement with the British Government; and that the British Government shall be entitled to land additional submarine cables or establish additional wireless stations for communication with places outside Ireland.

(b) That lighthouses, buoys, beacons, and any navigational marks or navigational aids shall be maintained by the Government of Ireland as at the date hereof and shall not be removed or added to except by agreement with the British Government.

(c) That war signal stations shall be closed down and left in charge of care and maintenance parties, the Government of Ireland being offered the option of taking them over and working them for commercial purposes subject to British Admiralty inspection, and guaranteeing the upkeep of existing telegraphic communication therewith.

In addition, in the course of the Dáil Cabinet's discussions *before the Treaty,* Mr. de Valera had put forward the following as the sort of oath he would agree to:—

"I, ..., do swear to bear true faith and allegiance to the Constitution of Ireland and the Treaty of Association of Ireland with the British Commonwealth of Nations, and to recognise the King of Great Britain as Head of the Associated States."

CORRECTIONS

(by P. S. O'Hegarty)

Page 6 and Page 13. All the untried prisoners, including Griffith, were released at Christmas, 1916. It was the sentenced prisoners only, including de Valera and MacNeill, who were retained until the middle of 1917.

Pages 26–27. The three happenings here given as the starting points of the attacks on different sections of the British forces are not in chronological order. The Soloheadbeg ambush was the earliest—21st January, 1919. The attacks on detectives in Dublin began with the shooting of Detective Sergeant Smith on 30th July, 1919; while Quinless, the first of the civilian spy cases, was shot on February 19th, 1920.